Community Dispute Resolution, Empowerment and Social Justice:

The Origins, History and Future of a Movement

Community Dispute Resolution, Empowerment and Social Justice:

The Origins, History and Future of a Movement

by Paul Wahrhaftig

NAFCM Press 2004

NAFCM
1527 New Hampshire Ave. NW
Washington DC 20036-1236
USA
www.nafcm.org | nafcm@nafcm.org

NAFCM Press is a project of The National Association for
Community Mediation. NAFCM is a membership-based
organization that supports the maintenance and growth of
community-based mediation programs and processes and
represents the interests of community mediation programs
and practitioners. NAFCM facilitates information exchanges
among its members, provides technical assistance to
community mediation centers, and advocates the use
of collaborative problem solving and community-based
conflict resolution.

FIRST EDITION

Printed in the United States of America

Library of Congress Control Number: 2004117424
ISBN 0-9763739-0-4

DEDICATION

I wish to dedicate this book to my committed friends Ursula and Robert Jaeger whose steadfast belief that individuals of good will can make a difference has sustained me for many a year.

TABLE OF CONTENTS

PREFACE

I have had the rare privilege of being a participant observer in the birth, growth, and maturation of a social movement, the Community Dispute Resolution (CDR} movement. For over thirty years I chronicled the growth and changes in this field. My institutional bases over the years were The Pittsburgh Pretrial Justice Program, the Grassroots Citizen Dispute Resolution Clearinghouse, (both projects of the American Friends Service Committee,) and the Conflict Resolution Center International. It all started in 1973 when I published a student written article advocating for a community forum to handle conflicts that otherwise might go to court. Subsequently, in the three quarterly periodicals I edited (The Pretrial Justice Quarterly, The Mooter, and Conflict Resolution Notes), and in my consulting role, I sought to give voice to those struggling with the community building potential of CDR programs. These organizers and researchers felt that the real potential of CDR programs transcended the individual disputes involved. They could be a tool for empowering communities and creating a culture of peace. That proposition is the main focus of this book.

Linda Baron, Executive Director of National Association for Community Mediation, (NAFCM), and others, have asked me to write what I have observed and learned from my unique, lengthy, involvement. "We need to know where we came from" was the way they phrased it. I feel that we need to know where we are going. I hope this historical view stimulates creative thinking about the future.

I hesitated to write because I am all too aware that over the course of my involvement the conflict resolution field has changed significantly. In the beginning, there was no literature for the field. We had to borrow articles from management, psychology, and other disciplines. It was easy for me to write the first handbook for organizers of CDR programs and have a major impact since there were no other publications available. Now there is more published in this field than anyone can keep up with. I know this with authority since I spent 30 years developing an extensive library on community dispute resolution that is now housed at the Conflict Resolution Network, Canada (annotated index available on their website http://www.crnetwork.ca).

I became convinced that even with this plethora of available publications, I have something important to say that is not yet in print. I began writing with a vision of keeping alive the community and peace building potential of CDR programs. My observation had been that while many of the founders were convinced that besides settling individual disputes, CDR programs could have a significant role in bringing about positive social change. My concern was that a common phenomenon in organizational development was taking place, namely, a transition from programs run by the founders to more mature programs run by maintenance oriented directors. As the founders, who are focused on the vision of the organization inevitably drop out of the field, the newer generation of program directors is more geared to organizational maintenance and smooth service delivery..

Is this phenomenon what Ann Weisbrod, one of the founders of the Institute for Mediation and Conflict Resolution's CDR program referred to in 1980, "I wonder if twenty years from now we will be meeting to develop an alternative to community dispute resolution?"

During my research I discovered that the question was much more complicated than "Does or does not the project help build community"? Instead of trying to revive the techniques of social change preferred by the originators, promoting community organizing programs, some programs are experimenting with a variety of ways to affect social change. I have tried to capture the breadth of this social movement.

The concepts the CDR field has wrestled with over the years are not peculiar to mediators. Rather, the themes are applicable wherever people are working towards empowerment. An important sub-theme in this work is an examination of the many levels in which questions of race intersect with CDR. In particular I touch on the lengthy process by which some CDR programs and resource centers began through the efforts of predominately white, educated people. Gradually and painfully CDR people learned to reach out and involve people of color, struggling with the move from salt and pepper integration to full inclusiveness. This process alone should be the subject of a book.

As it is, this work has evolved into a combination of approaches. While it tells the story of the CDR movement, it is far from a definitive history. It is the history as I saw and experienced it. It is somewhat autobiographical, built on what I have learned from my own involvement in the field. It does not cover the many excellent projects that I had not worked with or visited. I will feel it is a success if it stimulates creative thought about how to implement the potential that CDR programs have to strengthen communities and promote peaceful relationships.

ACKNOWLEDGMENTS

So many people have helped me to bring this book to publication. I can only cite a few who played a pivotal role.

Doga Akinci's painstaking reorganization and indexing of documents that might be relevant to this project gave me an important base to begin researching. Deborah S. Drezner, who helped me through writers block, drafted first drafts of some sections and helped refine others. Janet Seltman for her caring and precise editing assistance.

A stimulating group of people have read and commented on various drafts of this work. They are, Kim Bobrowsky, Linda Baron, Christopher Mitchell, Rosemarie Schmidt, Judy Shopp, Lawrence Suskind, Bill Warters, and Leah Wahrhaftig Jeri. Additional contributions were made by Dean Peachey, Peter Bruer, and Nathalie Rockhill in conducting a workshop for the Network for Conflict Resolution, Canada based on drafts of this book. Todd Sanders created the cover design, book layout, and steered me through the maze of publishing.

None of the work would have been possible without the strong encouragement I have received over the years from my wife, Scilla Wahrhaftig,

CHAPTER 1 — SOCIAL CLIMATE

It is important to remember that community mediation arose at a time when activism flourished in areas such as reform of the justice system, civil rights, feminism, community empowerment, self-help, voluntarism (Peace Corps, VISTA), and consensual problem solving. Many threads were woven together to form a new fabric. The federal government was willing to play a major role in supporting the growth of such efforts through grants backed by guidelines calling for community involvement and equitable representation.

– Albie Davis, 1991 [1]

Today there are literally hundreds of community dispute resolution (CDR) programs throughout the United States. However, as recently as 1973 you could count the number of these programs on one hand and still have fingers left over to stir your coffee. Many of the early dispute resolution programs were developed to serve as vehicles for promoting community change. As the field expanded the sense of CDR programs being a part of a social movement appears to have become diluted. That social change orientation needs to be revisited. Is community empowerment no longer on the CDR agenda? Or is it being expressed in different ways?

I use CDR to refer to programs that seek to resolve interpersonal disputes, whether criminal or civil, outside of the courts. Most often they use mediation as a non-coercive process although some use a combination of mediation and arbitration. The mediators often are volunteers. The term "community" was never defined precisely. In some programs it was a reference to an ethnic community, like the African American Community, while in others it was a neighborhood, a portion of a city, such as a precinct, or the whole city.

To understand CDR as a movement we need to remind ourselves of the social climate of the 1960s and 1970s, for here we will find the roots that nourished and shaped the early CDR programs. In 1990 I was serving on the Board of Directors of the Academy of Family Mediators (AFM), the professional association of divorce and family mediators. One evening, the informal conversation turned to, "Where were you in the 1960s"? Every member of that board had been active in either civil rights or peace work. If that common background was true of the very professional AFM, the attitudes of the 1960s and 1970s must have shaped the community dispute resolution movement even more profoundly.

Civil Rights

The 1960s was a period of turmoil, but more so of hope. The Kennedy administration rested on and enhanced a spirit of change and activism. The Peace Corps was one manifestation of the spirit that committed individuals can be catalysts for constructive and peaceful change.

The inequities of racial segregation had moved up on the national agenda after the 1954 *Brown vs. Board of Education* decision called for desegregation of the public schools. Resistance to integration of schools and public facilities had stalled progress throughout the 1950s. However, an organizing base was being laid in the late 1950s which would blossom in the early 1960s, as black and white citizens began to discover that everyday people working together can bring about positive change. Two examples follow. In 1955, the black community of Montgomery, Alabama boycotted segregated municipal buses for months. The effort resulted in integrated buses and the emergence of Dr. Martin Luther King Jr. as a prominent spokesperson for civil rights. In 1960 students organized sit-ins, desegregated lunch counters in Greensboro NC, and established the Student Non-violent Coordinating Committee (SNCC). People of all races and classes joined with southern blacks in freedom rides, demonstrations, voter registration, teaching in freedom schools to challenge inequities of segregation. They found that they could bring about change.

However, change did not come easily. Many civil rights activists were arrested and spent time in Southern jails and prisons. Many were beaten and killed. This exposed middle class white Americans to the inequities of society as a whole and particularly to the way the criminal justice system treated black Americans.

By the late 1960s, the Civil Rights movement was evolving rapidly. Whereas the early movement was built on the principle of blacks and whites working together, a new perspective of "Black Power" emerged, and soon came to dominate the movement. One of its fundamental premises was that blacks needed to organize their own liberation. The supporting role of whites was to work in their own communities to eliminate racism and remove the barriers to black progress.

As Black Power became a dominant force, the roles for blacks and whites working together became constricted. One area remained open: the criminal justice system. Courts, jails, and prisons were so insulated from the rest of society that it would require broad involvement to have any impact on them. So, many white civil rights workers gravitated towards criminal justice reform work.

My Civil Rights Background

My history and experience are representative of these trends. In 1965, I left my law practice in California and volunteered with the American Friends Service Committee (AFSC), a Quaker social action organization. I joined a team of young people who would spend the summer in small South Carolina towns that had been bypassed by the civil rights movement and remained segregated. We would tutor the first black children to integrate the local, more privileged, white schools.

My experience there confirmed my sense that change is possible and that I could play a role. When I asked some of the 11th and 12th grade students what job they wanted to prepare themselves for, they all answered that they would attend a traditionally black college and become a beautician, social worker or teacher. These were the traditional roles open to African Americans.

I sought to widen their horizons to take advantage of the changes that were taking place in society. I arranged a field trip to the University of North Carolina where my students met with a group of black students who were among the first to attend that formerly all white university. Ten years later I learned that from that little group of high school students one became an attorney, another an engineer, another a plant manager. One day in 1978 I telephoned for a reservation on Delta Airlines. The woman processing my request turned out to be one of the group from the summer of 1965.

I went on to work for the Georgia Council on Human Relations, an Atlanta based bi-racial civil rights organization. In 1967, I responded to the Black Power movement's call for whites to work in their own communities to reduce racism, by moving over to the Anti-Defamation League of B'nai B'rith, a Jewish defense agency which at that time was quite supportive of civil rights.

In both agencies I frequently found brochures and pamphlets on how to organize communities effectively, how to file civil rights complaints with the US Justice Department, how to document minimum wage violations and other civil rights and economic issues. I sent these back to the african-american civil rights leader who had hosted me for the 1965 summer project. With this information he desegregated all the public facilities in town and began work on economic issues, such a minimum wage. Overnight a town in the backwater of civil rights came up to speed.

I was only able to articulate the primary lesson I learned from this experience many years later, nevertheless it set me on my course. I learned that a useful role for me was providing the right information at the right time, enabling people to bring about change.

Vietnam War Opposition

During the same period, America's engagement in Indo-China grew into a prolonged war in Vietnam. Opposition to the war grew into a full-fledged peace movement that convulsed campuses across the country. Participants in the peace movement shared an outlook with civil rights – they wanted to remedy a terrible evil, but with a sense of hope that peace was a reachable goal. On April 4, 1967 Martin Luther King Jr. linked the two movements in his Riverside Church speech:

> Now it should be incandescently clear that no one who has any concern for the integrity and life of America today can ignore the present war. If America's soul becomes totally poisoned, part of the autopsy must read "Vietnam." It can never be saved so long as it destroys the deepest hopes of men the world over. So it is that those of us who are yet determined that 'America will be' are led down the path of protest and dissent, working for the health of our land.[2]

Peace activists shared the fate of many civil rights workers. Often they were arrested, jailed and, thus, given the opportunity to observe the excesses of the criminal justice system from the inside. This shared background led many from the peace movement as well as the civil rights movement to become involved in criminal justice reform.

My Anti-War Experience

While I did not play a leadership role in the peace movement, I did participate in anti-war activities, beginning with a major peace rally in San Francisco in 1964. I attended numerous peace demonstrations including the first one in the South and some at the Pentagon. I was in the audience in Atlanta when Dr King announced his opposition to the war for the first time in the South. The photo portrait I took of him that day has hung over my desk since his assassination.

Criminal Justice Reforms

By the mid-1960s, the criminal justice system was ripe for reform and change. A combination of social forces was at work. There was a significant group of idealistic activists who had experienced the excesses of the criminal justice system. Also, there was ferment from within the criminal justice system. A common complaint was that the system was overburdened. Courts had major backlogs, prisons were overcrowded, and virtually all procedures were getting bogged down. Some observers[3] suggested the real problem was that the courts were open to many first time users. Citizens brought civil rights suits, pursued employment discrimination claims, and used the available Legal Services attorneys to defend themselves from their creditors. The old users of the courts, mainly business related, looked for ways to divert these new users away from the courts to less expensive forums.

The bail reform movement demonstrates these trends. As peace and civil rights demonstrators were arrested, frequently the court would require the defendants to post bail to obtain their release. That meant they would have to put up a specified amount of money to guarantee their appearance at their trial. Some activists saw that this process inherently discriminated against the poor. Since the authorities tended to set higher bail for blacks than whites, it was yet another burden and indignity imposed on African Americans.

A couple of legal service/civil rights attorneys spearheaded a campaign to reform the bail system. They reasoned that the only legal purpose of bail is to assure appearance for hearings. They also understood that people who are well rooted in the community, indicated by having a stable residence, family, and employment, were fairly safe risks for release. No money deposit should be necessary as a guarantee. So, they encouraged the establishment of bail reform programs, measuring defendants' community roots and making recommendations to the appropriate judges.

My Bail Reform Activities

In 1969, US Steel Company began work on its home office building in Pittsburgh, Pennsylvania. The building trades at that time were unionized, and black workers found themselves excluded or only at the fringes of the unions. The new US Steel building became the focal point of demonstrations to open up the building trades to black workers. Daily demonstrations blocked access to the site and closed down the building project.

In the end, the black construction workers won access to the building trade job market. Demonstrations ceased, construction recommenced, and a major barrier to black employment was removed.

However, during the upheaval, many demonstrators, black and white, were arrested. Exorbitant bonds were set in an apparent attempt to wear down the demonstrators' resources. Angered by the injustice of this misuse of bail, some local Quakers approached American Friends Service Committee[*] to fund a project to reform the bail system in Pittsburgh. I was hired to implement that program. While inspired by the bail reform programs established in other cities, AFSC had its sights set higher. It wanted the community most aggrieved by the existing bail system to be actively involved in planning and implementing change.

I managed to form a coalition of African American community activists to study the bail system and previous attempts at reform. Our research documented that higher bail was set for black defendants than for white. We agreed that the idea of linking the judge's bail decision to

---

[*] The American Friends Service Committee, is a Quaker social service organization working for peace and social justice.

the strength of a defendant's community roots made sense. A person with a reasonably stable job, home address, and family is unlikely to flee from the jurisdiction. However, we observed that even in systems that had new bail reform agencies checking community roots, blacks were still subject to higher bail and detained at a higher rate than whites.

The problem, we determined, was that the definition of community roots was based on white middle-class assumptions: a steady residential address, a nuclear family and a job. Our group of activists could identify many black defendants who did not meet these criteria but were equally well rooted in the community and would not flee. A young man might not have his own apartment, might date several women, might not have a steady job, but could be found regularly hanging out at a certain street corner. People who live in the neighborhood have a sense of who is rooted there and who is risky.

Our solution was to organize a black community based bail program, which we called Community Release Agency (CRA). It was an independent non-profit corporation and received federal funding under the Law Enforcement Assistance Act. When a defendant was arrested from a CRA community, CRA staff from that neighborhood would check with reliable neighborhood contacts to gather information on the defendant's relationship to the community. This information would be summarized and presented to the bail setting authority. CRA would then follow up with the same contacts; to be sure the defendant knew when and where he was required to appear.

We did not invent CRA in isolation. As we were beginning to define the problem, I discovered several other community oriented bail reform efforts starting up in different parts of the state, including Chester, Media, and Philadelphia. I felt these fledgling programs could learn from and support each other as they struggled with their local bail situation. I obtained a small grant from the Pennsylvania Governor's Justice Commission* and put on a small statewide bail reform conference. Out of that conference evolved my next program, the Pennsylvania Pretrial Justice Program. That program, still an AFSC project, held conferences and published a quarterly periodical.

---

*The Pennsylvania Governor's Justice Commission administered funds granted from the federal government's Law Enforcement Assistance Administration. LEAA was the funding mechanism for the governments'War on Crime. While most of the funds went to strengthening police departments, some funds went to criminal justice reform projects.

I was able to distribute the publication nationally through AFSC's regional and national structure. Further, I attended conferences of the National Association of Pretrial Service Agencies (NAPSA), which was networking bail reform programs on a national level. NAPSA mailing lists opened up another source for national distribution of Pennsylvania Pretrial Justice Program materials.

CRA operated along the lines we envisioned for ten years, easing the plight of many black defendants. However, pressure from its funder, Law Enforcement Assistance Administration (LEAA), to become integrated with the criminal justice system, and the court's insistence on receiving more standardized quantifiable information, resulted in CRA being subsumed into the court system. Today, the bail system works nearly the same as it did before CRA started.

By 1973, I was confronted with a difficult situation. In four years I had achieved my initial goal of involving the Pittsburgh black community in designing and implementing bail reform. Also I had built a national network of community groups which were concerned with pretrial reforms, including bail. It became increasingly clear that the reforms were not working up to expectations. While those who would probably have been released on low bail before were released without bond, those who the court felt should not be released remained behind bars.

It was time for a change, for a new movement.

1. Albie Davis, "How to Ensure High Quality Mediation Services: the Issue of Credentialing," in *Community Mediation Handbook*, Karen Duffey, James W. Grovner, and Paul V Olczak, (eds.), Guilford Press, NY, 1991, p. 216

2. Martin Luther King, "Beyond Vietnam," April 4, 1967, http:www/ratical.com/ratville/ JFK/MLKapr67.html

3. For example, see, Mark H Lazerson, "In the Halls of Justice, the Only Justice Is in the Halls," *The Politics of Informal Justice*, Vol. 1, Richard Able, Ed., 1982, p. 120

CHAPTER 2 — IN THE BEGINNING

The failure of bail reform illustrates the *liberal's dilemma*. That is: liberals are fine at analyzing systems and defining the problems. However, when they invent solutions, implementation depends on the authorities in power agreeing with them.[1]

Frustrations of Criminal Justice Reform

This concept applies to bail reform because the judge always makes the final decision on bail. In making this decision, the judge may not agree with the risk assessment of the bail agency, even when knowledgeable community members vouch that their neighbor will appear in court. In the end, behind the window-dressing of these reformed bail agencies the community was no more empowered than it was before. The *liberal's dilemma* partially explains the tendency of alternative programs to mirror the institution that is to be reformed.

Juvenile Court is one of many examples in court history. It was originally founded to provide a softer, informal, more treatment oriented forum. Soon, due process issues came to the fore, children were granted the right to counsel, and juvenile court judges began to wear robes and to be seated on a raised platform. Today it is hard to see much difference between juvenile and adult court. I refer to this process as co-optation.

It was time to focus on a project that could work regardless of the opinions of the criminal justice authorities; a process that would actually shift decision-making power away from the courts and into communities. Michael J. Lowy, an anthropologist and member of the steering committee for the AFSC Pittsburgh Pretrial Justice Program formulated a concept that had the potential to work independently of the criminal justice authorities. In a keynote address to a Pennsylvania statewide pretrial justice conference that I arranged in 1972, he challenged the concept that so many disputes that turn up in courts are criminal in nature and ought to be judged on the basis of fault. Instead, he proposed that an informal process, similar to the "moots" he had studied among the Ashanti, in Ghana, might be used by neighborhood groups in this country to help residents deal with conflicts that arise within their own communities. Neighbors and friends in conflict should be able to settle their differences in an informal setting, focusing on the future – "how can we live together in peace," rather than battling over blame in the formalized court system.[*]

Lowy's presentation was so impressive and thought provoking that it did not seem right to go on with the rest of the conference agenda. Instead, the forty participants, over a few bottles of wine, changed the conference agenda so they could spend the whole period examining Lowy's proposal. This experience was what is now called "Open Conference Technology" - a planning approach that encourages conference attendees to structure the conference to fit their needs.

This event marked the beginning of my, and AFSC's, role in the Community Dispute Resolution (CDR) field. Using student researchers, I already had done a study that, when we reviewed it, helped confirm that it is possible to convert seemingly criminal situations into problems subject to informal settlement. In 1971, I conducted a research project to determine how Pittsburgh courts use bail. I used college students as court watchers. We compared bail-setting practices in a centralized downtown Magistrate's Court, in Pittsburgh, and in District Justices' offices in three ethnically distinct neighborhoods. The court watchers observed how bail was set for people charged with assault and battery or drug possession. The findings indicated that higher bail was set for blacks than whites and for poor than affluent citizens.

An unanticipated finding was that when the case appeared in a District Justice's small courtroom, the parties were much more likely to find a way to settle the case out of court rather than continue to process it as a criminal complaint. The frequency of these informal

---

[*] I heard this analysis in a talk given by Stanford Law Professor Richard Danzig, speaking at an informal colloquium, University of Pittsburgh Anthropology Department in 1972.

settlings did not vary significantly by either race or economics. Although "informal settlements" were worked out frequently in the small neighborhood District Justice's office-courtroom, they were rare in the crowded Magistrates' Court downtown. As we considered Lowy's "moots" we drew the conclusion from this study that it is possible to bypass the criminal justice system by helping the parties find a mutually acceptable settlement.

As we examined this new idea, reformers within the criminal justice system were also examining the possibilities of using informal, neighborhood dispute mechanisms to increase the efficiency of the court system. In 1965, a Presidential Commission on Law Enforcement and the Administration of Justice focused national attention on the overburdened judiciary. Its findings helped build consensus for the need for reform and experimentation in the court system, with particular focus on minor criminal cases involving neighbors, relatives and other acquaintances.[2]

Soon, prominent criminal justice officials also began calling for a community role in handling minor disputes. Chief Justice Warren Burger, in a 1977 address to the American Bar Association National Conference on Minor Disputes Resolution, drew on the observations of legal anthropologists and pointed to the need to consider adopting informal, neighborhood-type alternative dispute mechanisms, be they arbitration, mediation, or conciliation, to avoid expensive and lengthy legal proceedings in minor neighborhood disputes.

> The consumer with $300 in controversy …[is] more likely to go to a local neighborhood tribunal and would prefer one lawyer surrounded by two non-lawyers rather than a black-robed judge. The decision-makers must be trained or natural, practical psychologists, with an abundance of the milk of human kindness and patience.[3]

Notice that in this formulation, Chief Justice Burger reveals that he did not trust the process entirely to people outside of the court system, even as he espoused the idea of informal dispute resolution mechanisms. His suggestion that an attorney should be on the hearing panel would help keep the new forums under control. Thus, from the beginning two different philosophies drove efforts to establish community dispute resolution centers. Reformers based outside the criminal justice system thought in terms of empowerment of individuals and/or the community. Those within the criminal justice system saw it as a way to clear overburdened court dockets. This divergence of philosophies led to a conflict within the field that continues today.

My focus was on the community empowerment potential of conflict resolution organizing. This approach was consistent with AFSC's position paper on criminal justice reform in general, published as *Struggle for Justice*.[4] Community run dispute resolution centers have the potential to:

1. reduce the number of acts considered crimes committed by and upon people who have on-going relationships, and

2. increase the role of the community through its participation in these disputes by providing a mechanism for neighborhood members to examine and solve problems affecting their community.

The first criterion involves a conceptual and definitional shift in the understanding of criminal behavior. A large number of cases involving acts committed by and upon people who know each other would be diverted away from the criminal justice system. The second criteria values empowering disputing parties to make decisions about their disputes in the context of their communities. It is the neighborhood, rather than a courtroom judge that would enable this empowerment.

The conceptual division was not just theoretical, and it existed from the very first CDR projects. In 1973, as we digested Lowy's moots and planned a pilot project to test whether a CDR center designed to empower the community could work, we discovered that there were three programs already in existence. They ranged from purely community based to an agency model and finally one run entirely from within the criminal justice system. Since these three models existed already, we chose to study them instead of establishing our own center. We would see what we could learn from their experience and use that information to guide the future directions of our program.

Community Model

The Community Assistance Program in Chester, Pennsylvania developed the first community based dispute resolution program. The Community Assistance Program began as a project of the Philadelphia Yearly Meeting (Quakers).* In the 1960s, the Philadelphia Yearly Meeting had established a community center in Chester, an industrial, working-class community in which the majority of residents were African American. Eventually, in response to a takeover of the center by the black community who believed that white reformers should work in their own communities, the Quakers ceded the community center property to the black community.

Immediately the Friends established another Quaker peace and justice center in a barn behind a suburban Friends Meeting House in affluent, predominately white, Media, Pennsylvania. The new center was called the Friends Suburban Project. Some of the staff, that had attended the state-wide conference at which Lowy spoke, started a community dispute resolution program. It focused on problems of troubled youth. The Friends quickly developed their own capacity to train volunteer mediators, based on the Yearly Meeting's experience working with and training Peace Brigades. Peace Brigades were used overseas to help stave off civil violence. They were active, also, in Philadelphia during the 1960s and early 1970s, a period of major civic unrest. They helped monitor demonstrations to keep communications open or served as a buffer between organizers and police, between demonstrators and hecklers, and the like. Much of their training involved listening skills, reframing demands into problem statements, and defusing anger. With Peace Brigade organizer Charlie Walker occupying office space with Friends Suburban Project, it was natural to use his experience to develop mediation training.

Over the next few years, the Friends Suburban Project played a major role in providing mediation training throughout the Middle Atlantic region. They offered training at a cost that newly organized programs could manage, which meant that often they trained free or just charged for actual expenses. Their training became grounded in their growing experience as they continued to operate their own community mediation program in the suburbs. They documented their work well so others could benefit from their experience and were generous in sharing their training techniques. Their training manual, *The Mediator's Handbook*,[5] first published in 1982, is still on the market and is a classic.

---

* In Quaker practice, there is no hierarchy, but there are individual organizational units called "monthly meetings." They, in turn, belong to a regional federation, a "yearly meeting." In Philadelphia, the Yearly Meeting is staffed and runs projects.

When the black community took over the Community Assistance Program, it continued to work on criminal justice issues, such as bail reform. Laurice Miller, a staff member, was a very "motherly" woman to whom people naturally took their troubles. This role was an organic outgrowth of Community Assistance Program's activities because, as an observer explained,

> In this town of 50,000, one half of which is black, Diane Palm, Community Assistance Program director, and Laurice Miller either know everybody in the black community or they know how to reach them. For instance, when an electric typewriter was stolen from the office a few years back, Community Assistance Program put out the word. Within a day the thief returned the typewriter with his apologies.[6]

Miller caught the eye of a proposal writing consultant who was in the office for the day. He saw her talk with a group of people who, when they entered, were in a heated argument. Though they could not speak to each other civilly, when they left they were reconciled and at peace. The proposal writer observed that Miller had settled a case that otherwise would have gone to criminal court. He decided to call Miller a "mediator" and see if he could get her position funded through the newly organized federal War on Crime funding agency, the Law Enforcement Assistance Administration (LEAA). He succeeded, and this program became the first mediation program in the country to receive federal funding. However, the program never grew beyond this one woman, and when she moved to Florida, the mediation program ended. The importance of the Community Assistance Program, however, was that it affirmed the legitimacy of dispute resolution programs, both in terms of funding potential and the idea that problem solving is not the sole province of the legal profession.

Court System Model

Meanwhile, a court-operated program emerged in Columbus, Ohio. John Palmer, a law professor at Capitol Law School, designed it in 1971 in response to an overburdened court calendar. The authorities felt that too many people were filing private complaints. Often complainants would settle their disputes before their scheduled hearings and not bother to appear in court. Thus the court calendar became clogged with "no show" cases.

The prosecutor's office suggested charging complainants a fee to file a case which would be returned if they appeared at the scheduled hearing. Others, including Palmer, thought that approach was counter-productive if the goal was to reduce caseloads. So, Palmer proposed that these cases first be assigned to mediation. The sessions would be scheduled promptly, to be held in evenings at the Prosecutor's office. His law students would serve as mediators. The program became known as the Night Prosecutor.

When I observed the program in 1974 I found its form of mediation troubling. While mediation is voluntary and the mediator has no power to coerce an agreement, I saw that the mediators relied on a bundle of justice system symbols of authority. For instance, the document sent to the respondents to notify them of the mediation session was labeled a "subpoena". I reported on how these symbols of authority impacted the proceedings:

> The ability to go upstairs and write out a warrant on the spot is only one of the trimmings of authority upon which the program relies. All staff interviewed stressed the importance of authority. The symbolism of the flag, book cases full of law books, "subpoenas" and the like all serve an important purpose. Particularly tough cases may be mediated in the chief prosecutor's office, which has these trappings.
>
> Palmer feels these indicia of authority fulfill the complainant's need for his "pound of flesh." If the program just told the complainant they would call in the accused to talk things over and try to settle it, the complainant would be very frustrated. This way they get the satisfaction of seeing a "subpoena" issued and having the case "brought downtown."
>
> On the other hand, this approach can backfire. One session I observed had no trouble settling the main issue. However, the "accused" was so irate at having been "falsely accused", "charged", and "subpoenaed" that she demanded vindication. The case remained unresolved.[7]

Palmer's comment about the complainant wanting "his pound of flesh" has a basis in research. Anthropologists Sally Merry and Susan Sibley surveyed users of community mediation programs in New England and found that most complainants were looking for someone to agree that they are right, the other party is wrong and that they should be protected.[8] This disjuncture between many peoples' desire for a judgmental disputing process and CDR organizers' interest in establishing consensual processes is seldom discussed in much depth. The Night Prosecutor program apparently accepted the retributive motivation as a beginning and structured the program to satisfy those needs at least initially. Other programs paid less attention to the complainants' expectation and sought to draw the parties into a consensual process from scratch.

While the Night Prosecutor program was effective in settling many cases and reducing the court overload, I found it to be problematic. Law students with no mediation training are ill equipped to mediate. The logic of the two fields is quite different. When given a set of facts, the lawyer's job is to break the situation down into elements that will fit relevant categories. For example, is it a contract or a tort? The answer to that will lead to the next category, each repetition of this process narrows down the search to a point where an answer can be found. Mediators, on the other hand ask open-ended questions so they can understand the breadth and context of the problem. I recorded an example in my article, *Strengthening Communities Through Community Dispute Resolution Programs*.

> A real estate transaction involved a young man suing his uncle and aunt. The facts were rather illogical, and at one point he declared, 'I am going to get you to pay for this just like I did my other aunt.' He also talked about his "independence" from his mother who should "not be considered a part of my real estate transactions". No attempt was made to probe into these areas. The hearing focused on the real estate.[9]

This approach was appropriate from a legal logic perspective but not from a mediator's.

In short, my criticism of the Night Prosecutor program was that it was designed to meet the needs of the court and not the community. With the authoritarian trappings and legal focus of the program, individual parties were unlikely to feel empowered to resolve their conflicts or to learn how to resolve them better in the future. And certainly it did not enhance the problem solving capacity of the community. Those elements were simply not the court's business and hence not the Night Prosecutor's business.

Eventually the program added training for its mediators, and the quality of mediation improved. Recently, I have come to believe the Night Prosecutor was more beneficial to the entire community mediation field than I had given it credit. It helped mediation gain acceptance within the legal system. Since almost all attorneys in Columbus who graduate from Capitol Law School participate in the Night Prosecutor Program, most local attorneys have some experience with mediation. In the late 1970s the program was replicated in many other jurisdictions, particularly in the Mid-West.

Agency Model

The American Arbitration Association (AAA) has been a pioneer in the arbitration and mediation field since the early 1900s, handling commercial transactions, negligence cases, contract disputes and more. In the early 1970s they opened the 4A Program (Arbitration as an Alternative) in Rochester, NY, and soon afterwards started similar programs in Philadelphia and San Francisco. One observer, Edgar Dunn, described the program's standard procedure based on his observations of the Philadelphia program:

> If an individual has been robbed, beaten, or harassed by someone he/she knows, he/she goes to the Philadelphia Municipal Court and attempts to bring a criminal complaint against this person. Much to the surprise of the complaining party, she/he is informed that he/she and the other party may be assigned a day to meet at the [AAA] National Center for Dispute Settlement for an arbitration session.
>
> Although the "complainant" can pursue the matter through the usual court channels, he/she is encouraged to sign a "Submission to Arbitration" form.[10]

If the parties come to an agreement, the arbitrator writes it up like a mediation agreement. If they do not, the arbitrator decides the case. This two-fold approach came to be known as med/arb.

Typical of an "agency model", this program is housed outside of the court in a pre-existing organization that usually is responsible for activities other than the dispute center. In the 4A program it was housed in an agency that primarily conducted commercial arbitration. Later agency programs were housed in bar associations, neighborhood centers, and victim services agencies. The facility housing the agency program may or may not be located near to where the disputants live. The 4A program used a centralized location selected for its "other" activities: typically, in a business district. Usually, these dispute resolution programs received the bulk of their cases directly from the courts. The intervenors were not representative of the neighborhoods from which the parties came. If intervenors found out that they knew the parties or lived in the same neighborhood, they would have to disqualify themselves. The object of this policy was to protect mediator impartiality.

The 4A programs were well run and publicized. They provided another step forward in legitimizing mediation outside of the legal profession. The original Rochester program still exists in 2004, but is now independent from AAA. It is now called the Center for Dispute Resolution.

Thus, by 1973 three basic models of community dispute resolution programs had emerged: court, agency and community-based. All three helped people in conflict find a way to settle out of court. Over time, as the definition of agency was never clearly distinguished from community or court based models, this three part classification dropped out of use. So, for instance, the Rochester program which began as a model "agency" program now participates actively in the National Association for Community Mediation. The differences among the programs may be understood best by examining who becomes empowered in the process. We will examine empowerment more closely in Chapter 5.

1. Lowy, Michael J., *Basic Assumptions of Bail Reform and Pretrial Diversion – Some Alternatives*, Mimeograph by American Friends Service Committee, Pretrial Justice Federation, 1972

2. Scott Bradley and Melinda Smith, Community Mediation: Reflections on a Quarter Century of Practice, *Mediation Quarterly, Summer 2000*, Vol. 17, No. 4, p. 315

3. Warren E. Burger, "Our Viscous Legal Spiral", *The Judges Journal*, Vol. 16, No. 4, Fall 1977, p. 48

4. *Struggle for Justice: A Report on Crime and Punishment in America*. Prepared for the American Friends Service Committee. Hill and Wang, 1971

5. Jennifer E. Beer, Eileen Stief, *The Mediator's Handbook*, 3RD Edition, New Society Press, 1994

6. Paul Wahrhaftig, "Disputes Resolved in the Community," *Pretrial Justice Quarterly*, Vol. 2, No. 2, 1973, p. 1

7. Paul Wahrhaftig, "Mediation at the Police Station," *Pretrial Justice Quarterly*, Vol. 3, No. 4, Fall 1974, p. 1

8. Sally Merry and Susan Sibley, "What Do Plaintiffs Want?" *Justice Journal*, Vol. 9, No. 2, 1984

9. Op. Cit., Wahrhaftig, 1973

10. Dunn, Edgar, "Arbitration as an Alternative to District Courts," *The Citizen Dispute Organizer's Handbook*, Paul Wahrhaftig, ed., 1981, p. 30

CHAPTER 3 — EMPOWERMENT ÉTUDES

Community Dispute Resolution Programs (CDR), like most social change projects, can be viewed as icebergs. The service delivery aspect is the 10% of the iceberg visible above water, including the mediations, training and related support services. Hidden from view, however, are the empowerment issues. The entity that "owns" the program is likely to derive benefits from it. *Figure A* lists some of the gains that may be derived from a CDR program. These elements of empowerment will be discussed extensively in this chapter.

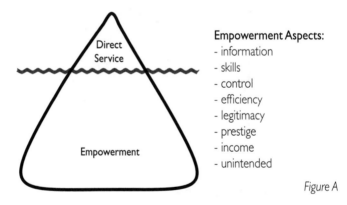

Empowerment Aspects:
- information
- skills
- control
- efficiency
- legitimacy
- prestige
- income
- unintended

Figure A

Since empowerment of somebody or some institution is inevitable in a successful program, I believe that communities should be strengthened by CDR programs, rather than courts or other controlling government institutions. However, that does not happen automatically; it must be planned carefully.

Figure B illustrates some elements of the community that may be empowered if the direct services are structured to do so. The program may aim at improving the community by strengthening community organizations, or by building up the CDR program's own ability to organize around community issues. It may help the disputants to knock on the doors of city hall for changes in policy that affect their dispute. It may promote a culture of peace. It may combine empowerment approaches. But if the empowerment issues are not considered in advance, the project may well empower the state to expand its web of control.

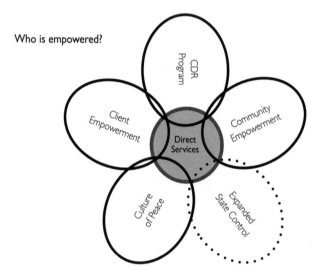

Who is empowered?

Figure B

These empowerment issues need to be examined in detail.

"Empowerment" Defined

Empowerment was a popular term during the civil rights period but is used only infrequently today. I use it here to describe a major element of the social change potential of CDR programs. Empowerment is a process with a number of components or elements such as improving people's ability to identify the nature of the problems they face, increasing their capacity for being heard, discovering relevant ideas and information about how problems might be solved, increasing their ability to mobilize key people and resources in their community to tackle problems, and find courses of action that offer the hope of change. Empowerment can be understood best by examining some examples. We will explore empowerment applied to individuals, communities, and to society at large. Empowering one level of society may be a route to empowering others.

Unfortunately "empowering" sounds like the empowerer is giving power to the recipient. Rather the empowerer helps people to release and use their own power. Many of us have had an empowering experience or relationship. Often the intervention takes the form of mentoring. If we reflect on successful empowering interventions in our own lives, we may be able to understand "empowerment" better in the CDR context.

Personal Empowerment Experiences

In the 1960s, two interventions in my life set me on the road that led, twenty years later, to creating an international network supporting conflict resolution work: the Conflict Resolution Center, International.

I graduated from law school in 1963 and began practicing law in 1964. I had taken an entry-level position in my father's former law firm. He had been dead for many years and two cousins ran the firm. Law and I did not get along. I was miserable and not working up to par. I would try to do legal research, but when I would open a book and start reading I would go into what I called a "white out". I would find that a half hour had lapsed and I was still looking at the first paragraph.

My cousin, recognizing earlier than I, that I was miserable and not a good personnel investment, suggested I talk to his friend Ted Terrail about my experience with law. Terrail, was a social worker and director of the Jewish Community Center in Oakland, California. In a single interview he helped me clarify that I did not want to practice law, and I really did want to help people directly through my work. Acknowledging those two points felt liberating. When I resigned from the law firm that afternoon, I felt empowered. I remember how buoyant I felt walking out of my father's law office and into my new life.

For me, empowering interventions were psychological. I had always felt locked into family expectations that had been expressed in many ways throughout my childhood. There was subtle pressure for me to join the family firm, which specialized in probate law. My father also taught me that wills and contracts must be written to "bullet-proof" so that future lawyers could not find weak spots in the document to challenge.

The importance of this empowerment experience was in letting go of the "be perfect" message and giving myself permission to seek my way of helping people. My search led directly to my involvement in the Civil Rights Movement.

Mutual Empowerment

One of the first things I learned when I went South was that empowerment is seldom a one way transaction. Both parties may benefit and grow from the experience. In 1965, I worked with Rev. J.D. McManus, a civil rights activist in Pageland, South Carolina. I had taken a volunteer assignment with the American Friends Service Committee to work with black children who would desegregate the "white" schools the following autumn. I was to tutor them in preparation for the more advanced white schools. I worked closely with Rev. McManus, whom I helped empower by providing information, contacts, and technical skills. But at the same time, he reinforced in me a sense of competence and assurance that I had never experienced before. One of his sayings still guides me. When I asked him how he coped with all the adversity he had confronted in his life, he told me, "You know, I don't have to keep my head above water, just my nose".

Another major lesson I received from Rev. McManus was that I could help others become empowered best through helping them acquire information and resources. After I left Pageland, I found I could be most effective, sitting in my office in Atlanta sending McManus how-to-do-it pamphlets and memos on civil rights issues. Once Rev. McManus had absorbed enough information, change came to Pageland rapidly. I, in turn, continued to create empowering networks among black and white small business owners, welfare recipients, criminal justice reformers, and finally, conflict resolvers.

Empowerment in CDR

Empowerment is not a static concept. Empowerment-oriented CDR programs evolved a spectrum of models. They ranged from ones that stressed empowering the individual parties to solve their own disputes, to the CDR program that advocated for change in the community based on information gleaned from individual case experiences. My own understanding of empowerment also evolved over the years. My evolution will become clear in the program descriptions that follow.

Coming to the idea of CDR programs from a criminal justice reform perspective, I saw these programs as a valuable service to the disputing parties. I understood that by anchoring ownership and control of the program in a community, one could help to insure that this useful service would not be co-opted and absorbed by the court system. I understood the empowerment potential mainly as empowering the parties to find their own solution to their problem and possibly to learn some negotiating skills for future use.

Empowerment of Individuals

The individual empowerment focus raised interesting training issues. In the 1970s, I studied the various training models available and found some more appropriate than others for individual empowerment. For example, consider the experience of the very first training at the Pittsburgh Mediation Center. In 1980, I was serving as a consultant to Deidre Levdansky as she developed a new CDR program. We hired a highly recommended trainer, Ernie Odom of the Suffolk County, (Coram) NY mediation program. He was an excellent, dynamic trainer. However, when Levdansky and I reflected on the training afterward, we agreed that although the experience was solid, it did not fit our sense of empowerment.

Odom's model relied heavily on private sessions with each of the parties. The process involved working with the parties together at the beginning so they could vent and hear each other. Then, through a series of private separate sessions with each party, Odom would narrow down the differences and solutions would emerge. When a settlement was nearly complete, he would reconvene a joint session at which the resolution would be introduced and approved.[*]

---

[*] Odom trained in an early version of the IMCR model (see Chapter 5.) In a 1979 issue of *Conflict Resolution Notes* ["A Response to Felstiner and Williams, Vol. 2, #2, p 36] George Nicolau, President of IMCR, indicated that they have been sensitive to criticism and have rethought the "direct" and "indirect" communication issue and "adapted our training accordingly." However, many trainers trained in IMCR's early model continued to pass on the unrevised model they had learned earlier.

Our concern was that an important dimension of empowerment lay in providing the parties with a learning experience, as they shape the solution to their own problem. From that experience they could see that they have the capacity to solve problems through communication rather than intimidation. Odom's approach, we felt, merely taught the participants that if they would have a difficult problem, they can bring it to an expert mediator who will guide them to a solution.

With that in mind, Levdansky and I retrained all the mediators in a model that stressed direct face-to-face communication among the parties. Direct communications, with the mediator serving as a coach, were designed to give the parties a chance to learn some basic skills, like the ability to assert one's needs constructively with "I messages," and the power of listening. We felt that these lessons were of more value to the parties, in the long run, than the agreement they reached on the initial problem. Mediators using this model could help empower individual participants to handle future conflicts on their own.

Empowering Neighborhoods for Change

In 1976, I was studying how a CDR program could move beyond empowering the immediate parties, to help build a community. This rather abstract and seemingly unrealistic concept became much more tangible and real when I met with Raymond Shonholtz and anthropologist Laura Nader. We met to critique Shonholtz's proposal to establish the San Francisco's Community Boards Program. It was designed to increase community knowledge and encourage involvement in neighborhood-wide problems. It sought ways for people to learn from individual conflicts about the problems facing their community. If, for instance, a series of conciliations revealed that the individual conflicts are symptomatic of a broader community problem, they could present that observation to existing neighborhood organizations. That information could both empower and prod the organizations to take more active roles in problematic areas.

I wrote of my doubts about this empowerment model in 1976. Shonholtz's Community Boards was in the proposal stage, close to starting up. Both he and I were struggling to understand community empowerment and how it could be implemented. After reviewing the proposal I wrote,

> [T]heir current proposal ... calls for setting up community boards
> before whom people appear for mediation or to be referred
> to social agencies. It seems to give the community more power
> than the kind of program we have been talking about. They can, in
> subtle ways, coerce people into taking part in rehabilitative
> programs ... Ray and I have gone back and forth on whether we
> are giving power, unchecked by due process safeguards to an un-
> elected sub-set of community members to impose uniformity – or
> is it that "empowerment of communities" is a liberal cliche, and
> we just really don't want communities to really have self-governing
> power?[1]

Soon after that discussion the Community Board role of referring
people to social agencies for treatment was de-emphasized.

After the program began operations, I observed an illustrative
case in 1979. Neighbors complained that one woman's house, in a
housing development, had been abandoned after a fire had damaged it
heavily. It was becoming a neighborhood nuisance, other homeowners
wanted it boarded up. Through controlled dialogue, the parties
discovered a city agency that would help the homeowner board the
house up and would offer advice on how to untangle an insurance
problem that had been blocking the house repairs. As they worked
through this individual situation, a spectator[*] observed that there had
been frequent fires in that subdivision because the builder had done a
substandard wiring job.

Suddenly what had been a dispute among a few individuals
became a community-wide problem. This added dimension provided
an opportunity for the neighborhood to work together to tackle
a problem of mutual interest. Although Community Boards was
designed to produce exactly this sort of empowering opportunity,
I discovered on return visits over the next two years that no one
had followed up to turn this information into collective action.

Individual Parties Promote Social Change

With my increased awareness of the potential a CDR program has
for building up the strength of community organizations, I began to

---

[*] Community Boards was unusual in the CDR field because it held its mediation sessions in public
to encourage broad participation and a wider opportunity to learn from the conflict at hand.

understand that programs could also have the goal of empowering the parties in the dispute to be of service to their communities. One such program was Community Association for Mediation (CAM) in Pittsburgh, Pennsylvania. Gloria Patterson, one of my AFSC committee members and later AFSC staff, organized a project that encouraged individuals to become involved in urban issues to promote change.

This approach is evidenced in a case study from CAM. This was a grassroots project located in Pittsburgh's central African American community, the Hill District. One of the program's mediators lived in a public housing development. She heard loud arguing outside her window and spotted two neighbors shouting at each other. The intensity was accelerating rapidly. Before the argument could escalate into violence, she went outside and invited the two angry women into her home to have a cup of tea and to talk about what was bothering them. The story began to emerge. Ms. A. lived on the first floor and accused Mrs. B's children, who lived upstairs, of knocking over garbage cans and strewing the contents all over the grounds. Mrs. B. denied that her children would do such a thing, but she did point out that one of her children's chores was to carry out the trash to the bins in the yard. After a little more talking and inquiry the two women agreed that the children were not purposely spreading trash. The problem was that there were too few garbage cans and the housing authority picked them up too infrequently.

The women agreed jointly to contact the housing authority to get more garbage cans and to step up garbage collection. Empowered with their new insights and information they contacted the authorities and were successful. Thus, an individualized complaint revealed a community problem. The parties were able to cooperate to achieve an outcome that benefited the entire community.

Parties Organize for Change

There are other empowerment possibilities. For example, the parties to a mediation may end up organizing themselves to lobby for community improvements. That happened in a dispute that arose between two "gangs"* of girls from two adjacent neighborhoods in

---

* Certainly there were two neighborhood clusters of girls. However, the girls did not define themselves as gangs. That was a characterization imposed by adults.

Pittsburgh, Pennsylvania. These groups regularly fought on the street, and eventually the fighting spilled over onto their high school campus. The Schenley High School authorities were unable to stop the skirmishes and called the Pittsburgh Human Relations Commission, which referred the school to the Pittsburgh Mediation Center.

The Center sent out a team of mediators to work with both groups of students. In separate private sessions, the intervenors discovered that no one knew what the conflict was about anymore. It had reached the point where the two groups were exchanging retaliations. It also became obvious that the girls shared a common frustration with the lack of recreational facilities in their neighborhoods and with the disciplinary methods used by their school. They asserted that inadequate recreational facilities made it all too easy for students to get into trouble. Further, when trouble broke out, they felt that suspending students only made matters worse.

The mediators brought the two groups of girls together in the school auditorium and conducted an intense group mediation process. The chairs tell the story of the mediation session. At the beginning the two groups of girls took seats on opposite sides of the room with their shoulders and back turned towards the "others". As the mediation progressed, the chairs gradually moved, seemingly spontaneously. By the end of the lengthy session the girls were sitting in a circle with girls from both neighborhoods intermingled.

In the end, the girls set up a joint team to lobby the city for expanded recreational facilities in their neighborhoods. Another team advocated establishing a peer mediation program in the school. Both teams were successful. Several new basketball courts and play facilities became available in the neighborhoods and the first peer mediation program in Pittsburgh was established in their school. Schenley High School's peer mediation program became the model adopted by the Pittsburgh school system. The Board of Education institutionalized it by creating a conflict resolution training and resource center available in all the schools. Thus, a single mediated situation empowered the parties to make institutional changes in their neighborhood and school.

Self-Empowering CDR Program

A step beyond the Community Board approach to community empowerment is the Cleveland Mediation Center, which empowers itself, as a neighborhood institution, to tackle community wide problems. The community center, where the program was located, was oriented towards advocacy. It used mediation as one tool to accomplish its goals.

When it first began operations it mediated disputes involving youth and was called the Cleveland Youth Mediation Program (CYMP). The mediations were expected to involve referrals to social service agencies. CYMP was to follow up to see that the services were really delivered. If they found a gap in service, that information would be brought to the CYMP board, which would advocate for change so the service would indeed be available.

That is exactly the way CYMP worked. An early accomplishment was documenting inadequacies in school truancy procedures, and successfully advocating for improvements. It is controversial for the program itself to lobby for change, rather than the parties or independent agencies. It flies in the face of concepts of mediator neutrality or impartiality. Dan Joyce, Director of the Cleveland center[*] responds, "Is it mediation? I don't know and I don't care. Our mission is to do conflict resolution work. That is a broader mandate than just mediation."[2]

A related question about this program is whether it is an empowerment program at all. Implied in the usual understanding of the term is the idea that there are separate entities: an empowerer and an empowered. Here they are the same organization. Daniel Joyce asserts that this approach is indeed a community empowering process. If the mission is empowering communities, and the Community Mediation Program is a community based institution, then community empowerment is taking place.

Individual Empowerment Nexus to Community Empowerment

By the mid-1980s the community and individual empowerment concepts came together. Many community mediation programs, recognizing that their caseloads were too low to attract funding, saw the answer in training. Others felt frustrated with the minimal impact of the community organizing approach to empowerment.

[*] Now known as the Cleveland Mediation Program since it now works with disputes among adults as well as youth.

> [The approach to community organizing of] "get together and bang
> on the doors of city hall" has not worked so much. The times we
> [in Canada] tried to use conflict as an organizing event to create
> community has only had a short-term impact. We had cases involving
> racial tension, beating with baseball bats, community tensions. As an
> outcome of mediation we agreed on establishing a fun day for
> kids and forming an organization. However, once the immediate
> incident and tension dissipated, the organization did not continue.
>
> When we take conflict resolution skills into community
> organizations, associations, and workplaces, we are having a greater
> impact on improving life and changing those institutions, but not
> necessarily the broader geographical community that we had
> hoped for in our vision.[3]

Pittsburgh Mediation Center (PMC) is a typical example. Until 1993
their raison d'être was to conduct mediations. People were trained in
sufficient quantities to fulfill the program's need for trained mediators.

Then the idea emerged that institutions consist of individuals. By
training many citizens in conflict resolution skills, one would be passing
on peacemaking skills and tools for democratic participation. A critical
mass of trained conflict resolvers could transform an institution or
community. Thus, PMC's understanding of its mission changed so that
handling cases and training the public became equal priorities.

This approach, of encouraging community change by training
large numbers of individuals, had considerable appeal in the 1990s.
It seemed more consistent with the attitudes of the overall society,
in which organizing collectively was de-emphasized and individualism
was valued. Further, this approach made economic sense for the
dispute resolution programs. They had been unable to charge, or bill a
significant amount for mediation sessions for two reasons. One was a
commitment to provide dispute resolution services to people lacking
funds to pursue their dispute through the traditional legal system.
Second, their competition as a dispute-resolving forum, the courts, are
accessible at no, or minimal, cost.* However, neither of these rationales
applies to providing training services. Training became a valuable
service that could be marketed to a broad spectrum of society
including institutions which CDR programs could charge reasonable

---

* Of course, if one relies on an attorney in either forum, their fees increase the cost
of disputing.

fees. Training has grown into an important income stream for many community dispute resolution programs.

Implicit in this emphasis on training is a reorientation beyond the original criminal justice alternative, towards a community building vision. These training programs are geared towards building a "culture of peace", and spreading democratic skills. The United Nations, in 2000, declared the year of Building a Culture of Peace. Widespread training in conflict resolution and problem solving, both essential democratic skills, was consistent with the UN goals.

School Mediation Programs

A logical extension of this training approach to empowerment was to focus attention on schools. If students could learn conflict resolution skills, they would become agents of change in the future. During the 1990s, federal funding was available for "violence prevention" programs, which was interpreted to include school mediation programs. This funding created a demand for training that many CDR centers were eager to fulfill. However, the demand for CDR training was short term because school systems tended either to drop the program when federal money was exhausted or to build an in-house training capacity.

By the late 1990s, school mediation programs were commonplace around the country. In 1997, I conducted a survey of 86 Western Pennsylvania school districts and found that almost every district had at least one conflict resolution program.

Empowering the Civic Body Through Dialogue

One way conflict resolution programs can help empower on a city wide basis (as opposed to a neighborhood) is by promoting and staffing dialogue groups. A leading example is the Lancaster Mediation Center, in Lancaster, Pennsylvania, which held its first city dialogue in 1996. I published an article written by Mark Siemen that described this foray by a mediation center into dialogue.

> One of the challenges of running a community mediation center is forging strong links to the community at all levels. Even more challenging is finding ways of addressing macro issues in the community, like racism and economic injustice.

Lancaster Mediation Center (Lancaster, Pennsylvania) Executive Director Grace S. Byler met with a small group of community leaders for two years to discuss the needs of the community and how the Center might have a role in addressing those needs. Over time the group homed in on the atmosphere of political battles in Lancaster County that made it seem impossible to have a civil discussion of differences of opinion.

A plan to invite all sectors of the community to a dinner emerged from these meetings. The idea was simple: bring people together to sit at tables of eight, each with a trained facilitator. Ask them to talk about the Lancaster City-County community, first by discussing what they like about the community, then by looking at aspects that need improvement. Encourage people to bring stories and answers from their unique backgrounds to community issues and problems.

After two years of dreaming and several months of intensive work on outreach and implementing the dream, the dinner was a joyous, celebrative evening of laughter and attentive listening. The actual attendance of around 300 was gratifying but short of the dream. We were happy for those people who did take the risk to come, and felt that their risk-taking was amply rewarded by energizing conversations.

Follow-up will include formation of general discussion groups and issue discussion groups based on preferences expressed that night.[4]

The dinner was so successful in opening interracial communications that some of the table-groups continued to meet throughout the year. The organizers repeated the program the following year.

Transformative Empowerment Distinguished

My use of "empowerment" is somewhat different from the way it is used in Bush and Folger's The Promise of Mediation[5], which, conceptualizes empowerment primarily as enabling the parties to change their relationship, and secondarily enabling them to find a solution to their problem. Folger and Bush introduced and popularized the transformative approach to mediation in which the mediator plays a seemingly passive role encouraging the parties to recognize and acknowledge each other and regain a sense of confidence and self-worth while discussing the conflict. The parties become empowered within the context of the mediation session and the conflict.

Folger commented on his motivation for encouraging this model:

> I am concerned that the value of empowerment is getting lost as
> many practitioners place major emphasis on reaching settlements
> and reducing caseloads. The very act of allowing disputants
> to attempt to construct an agreement in itself is the basis of
> mediation's unique empowerment. Empowerment can take place
> even if the parties fail to reach an agreement and thus do not
> reduce caseloads.[6]

It appears as if no transfer of skills to the parties is contemplated
much less any mention of having an impact on the community . From
the transformative perspective, it would be true that "no transfer
of skills to the parties is contemplated" because the parties are
considered to be able and capable to work out their own agreement,
if that is what they choose to do. The idea that there is only one or
a limited set of tools to reach agreement - and the parties do not
have those means or tools already - would be considered to be an
inherently disempowering perspective. Thus, the mediator would not
attempt to teach the parties any skills to use in crafting an agreement.

Kim Bobrowsky, a transformational mediation trainer, observed,

> As far as no "mention of having an impact on the community,"
> again from the transformative perspective, the community will be
> directly or indirectly affected because the parties, as members of the
> community, are becoming more self-reliant in working out disputes.
> The more empowered they become, the more "recognition" is likely
> to occur between members of the community, with a resultant
> increase in community harmony.
>
> Another way of saying this is that people become empowered
> by learning that they can make their own decisions and resolve their
> own disputes, which in turn is likely to increase their self-confidence,
> which in turn contributes to a more peaceful community.[7]

Empowering Society; Building a Culture of Peace

Empowerment can be applied to civic culture. Andrew M. Sachs
was a pioneer in involving CDR programs in mediating public policy
controversies. He developed the first training manual designed for
community mediators who work on complex, multiparty policy
disputes. He is on the staff of the Orange County Dispute Settlement

Center in North Carolina.* He referred to the growth in the use of community mediators as dialogue leaders, facilitators and mediators in major community-wide problem solving efforts

People who use consensus-based approaches to dispute resolution and find that they work become advocates of and advance the idea of consensus building. Many more citizens and public officials are gaining direct and positive experience in consensus-based public dispute resolution... As a result, community mediation centers are creating informed advocates for ...consensus processes in pubic affairs across the United States.[8]

A Canadian project defines its goal as "Spreading the 'Peace Virus'". The Ottawa-Carlton Neighborhood Coalition for Conflict Resolution established a grassroots dispute resolution program in Bellevue Manor, a tense neighborhood of low income housing in Ottawa. Volunteer mediators from the community are trained and sent back to the community infected with a "peace virus". The result is a major reduction in police calls to the neighborhood. The trained volunteers have found self confidence and jobs".[9]

The best example is overseas in Northern Ireland. Stimulated by the American experience the Northern Irish began to organize conflict resolution programs around 1986. None of these conflict resolution programs dealt directly with "the troubles", but organizers had a sub-agenda of fostering a culture of peace. In 1989, Joan Broder, then director of the Northern Ireland Mediation Council, described the empowerment of civic culture that was taking place.

> In three main ways I see our conflict resolution work as having a direct impact:
>
> First, is the Irish are learning that conflict can be positive and needs time. Living in a society where conflict is viewed as negative and to be avoided, this is a real mind shift for people. The training helps bring this about, so people can feel they can face conflict.
>
> Second, you are actually giving people skills, so they feel more confident and more equipped to deal with the conflict. They can use these skills not only in their professional life but in their working life, and for their personal lives as well.

---

* See Chapter 5 for the origins of the Orange County program, initially organized as the Carrboro Dispute Settlement Program.

The third area is the process itself. Those who are trained in conflict resolution skills, begin to see that there is a definite process that you must go through before you reach a solution. We are a very solution oriented society. We also tend to concentrate on the negatives rather than the positives. The training makes people realize that you have to create the right environment before you can ever move on to solution.

I believe that in Northern Ireland we are just at the stage of creating the right environment and that conflict resolution is a strand in this process.

It is a time of hope, but it should not be overestimated. I do not see the violence as going away for another five or 10 years, but I do believe that in the end we will get there.[10]

The Good Friday Accords were signed nine years later, in 1998, ushering in an era of relative peace. Strong public opinion, favoring peacemaking and resolving issues through negotiation rather than guns, helped push both sides to the table and to agreement. Since then, despite many attempts by politicians and militia on both sides to scuttle the agreements, they still hold. The recognition that one can deal with conflict over the negotiating table continues to drive public opinion, and makes it difficult for politicians and militias to take steps that would re-ignite violence.

This analysis should not imply that negotiating was alien to Irish culture. Quite the contrary. When I made my first trip to Northern Ireland, in 1981, the people I met promoting inter-communal understanding and peace all referred me to the public opinion polls. Although central Belfast was known for its bombed-out pubs and heavily fortified road-blocks, time after time public opinion polls showed that the majority of Northern Ireland's residents favored a peaceful settlement. However, when election day would come, they would not support the centrist parties, but would cast their ballot defensively with the extreme party representing their community. Perhaps the real role of the CDR programs was to convince the public that not only was a negotiated peace process theoretically an ideal way to handle the "troubles", but it actually might work.

Thus, while American CDR programs are training now in the hope that spreading conflict resolution skills broadly will transform their society and create a culture of peace, the Northern Irish have demonstrated that it can be done. The Irish success that I was privileged to participate in, through my networking activities at the Conflict Resolution Center International, crystallized my growing awareness that the CDR field was much more significant than I had originally thought. Yes, it is an alternative to the criminal justice system. Yes, it is a tool for empowering communities, but most important it is a workable peace program. It can empower the peacemakers.

A Note on Community

The "C" in CDR stands for "community." Community is a fundamental concept for the empowerment oriented program organizer, but rarely is it defined. Community empowerment organizers generally referred to "community" as a geographical entity smaller than a city. Ray Shonholtz, describing Community Boards, simply referred to "neighborhoods".[11] Others, such as the Community Association for Mediation, viewed community in terms of geography, economics and ethnicity, choosing a low income predominately black neighborhood. Gradually, over time, the sense of community broadened to include whole cities.

Just as the civil rights and community organizing activists of the 1960s seldom defined the "community" in community organizing, neither did CDR organizers. Ambiguity allowed organizers to write grant proposals that seemed consistent with various funders' definitions of community. One could receive funding from a civil rights oriented resource to work in the black community, and also solicit support for advancement of democratic skills from a local community fund that is uncomfortable funding racial issues.

By not defining "community", organizers avoided long discussions about the nature of "community". Do we simply belong to the community where we live? What about where we work or worship? Is the neighborhood a viable structure? Was it ever viable? However, the failure to have such discussions may have become a hindrance to the CDR movement, as we will discuss in Chapter 9.

We now have seen how the simple concept of empowerment, providing the tools, skills and opportunities that help people to exercise their influence in and beyond the particular conflict they face, can be implemented in many different ways. As my experience with these programs broadened, I became much more flexible in defining and advocating for establishing an "empowering" project. Community

Empowerment turned out to be a goal that could be reached by many paths, whether transferring skills to individuals, groups, or whole communities. We move now to examine the controversy over whether community empowerment is an appropriate goal for CDR programs.

1. Paul Wahrhaftig, *Letter to Mike Lowy*, October 19, 1976

2. Daniel Joyce, interview, December 13, 2002

3. Dean Peachey, Remarks made in workshop, *Strengthening Communities Through Community Dispute Resolution Programs at the conference Interaction 2004*, June 4, 2004

4. Excerpted from: "Community Forum for Civil Discourse," Mark Siemens, *Conflict Resolution Notes*, Vol. 14, No. 4, 1996, p. 1

5. Robert A. Baruch Bush and Joseph P. Folger, *The Promise of Mediation, Responding to Conflict Through Empowerment and Recognition*, Jossey-Bass, 1994

6. Joseph Folger, "Empowerment: Self Determination or Altruistic Persuasion?" *Conflict Resolution Notes*, Vol. 8, No. 1, 1990, p. 1

7. Kim Bobrowsky, E-mail message to Paul Wahrhaftig, June 3, 2004

8. Andrew M. Sachs, "Understanding Public Dispute Resolution in Community Mediation," *Mediation Quarterly*, Vol. 17, No. 4, Summer 2000, p. 343

9. Editor, "Spreading the 'Peace Virus'", *Ottawa Citizen*, p. D4, April 10, 1998, as posted at http://www.webnet/nccr/citizen.html

10. Joan Broder, "Mediation in Ireland," *Conflict Resolution Notes*, Vol. 6, No. 4, 1989, p. 79

11. Raymond Shonholtz, *The Citizens' Role in Justice: Building a Primary Justice and Prevention System at the Neighborhood Level*, Manuscript, 1987

CHAPTER 4 — DIVERGING PHILOSOPHIES

Throughout the 1970s and 1980s tensions abounded over the mission of CDR programs. Should they be concerned with "empowerment" beyond the immediate conflict or should they concentrate on managing cases efficiently? Court oriented programs were labeled as serving mainly the interests of the justice system. Community empowerment oriented projects tended to be dismissed as "1960's style social work".

Frank Sanders and Roger Fisher, Harvard Law School professors, were active in establishing court oriented models. Fisher had published *Getting to Yes*, the first book that popularized the basic concepts of collaborative dispute resolution. Sanders had pioneered gaining acceptance for court oriented dispute resolution programs and had become the American Bar Association's leading thinker and spokesperson on "Alternative Dispute Resolution".[*] One of Sanders' concepts was the "multi-door courthouse". Under that model, instead of cases immediately going to court or straight to mediation, an intake process would be established in which a court clerk would evaluate each case and assign it either to mediation, pretrial diversion or the court, as deemed appropriate. In Sanders' model, this "gatekeeper" would be administratively responsible to the court.

---

[*] Alternative Dispute Resolution (ADR) was a term lawyers applied to dispute resolution programs. Community dispute resolution organizers, including me, tended to reject the ADR terminology because it implied that the courts are the primary dispute mechanism. We felt that the courts were just one alternative, a back up, to be used after more informal mechanisms in the family and community had been tried. In this book I only use ADR in the context of court controlled programs – otherwise I use CDR (Community Dispute Resolution).

In contrast, Ray Shonholtz, founder of the San Francisco Community Boards Program, would locate the "gatekeeper" at the community level. "Civic work and commonality of work interests serve as social bonds . . . The more the community can of itself exercise its civic functions, the more the need for formal law is lessened."[1]

In the mid-1970s, I was invited to address a seminar at Harvard Law School and was introduced to the depth of this divide. Fisher and Sanders established a monthly seminar series on dispute resolution, attended by students faculty and some attorneys and judges. Their program, including this seminar, had become a "think tank" for the court-oriented dispute resolution world.

My topic was community dispute resolution, and I emphasized my conviction that volunteers could be competent mediators. It is not necessary (or even desirable) that all mediators be attorneys. Most of the participants could agree to that proposition.

I discussed the *liberal's dilemma*: The dilemma is that liberals are fine at identifying what is not working within an institution. They tend to devise solutions that are dependent on those already in power agreeing with them. However, those already in power are unlikely to change the system. The result is that change becomes illusory or temporary.

I explained my view that community based conflict resolution programs avoid the *liberal's dilemma*, since a CDR program can handle a case regardless of whether the court agrees that it is appropriate. Thus, at least theoretically, communities rather than the courts could be empowered to determine which disputes to handle in the neighborhood and which should go to court.

That was when I lost them. This idea seemed to shock the law professors and students at the seminar. Questioning became sharp and critical. I was queried on whether I was proposing substituting the whim of the public for the rule of law. The tone of the seminar quickly changed to an adversarial mode, and I felt I had to defend my community empowerment concept from attack.

Only one student understood me and seemed to agree with my approach. He was a young Yale divinity student named Ron Kraybill. He went on to found the Mennonite Conciliation Services and to play a major role in advancing the role of "non-professionals" in domestic and international mediation efforts.

How did this tension between advocates of differing models manifest itself on the ground? Advocates of community empowerment stressed the importance of CDR programs having a strong community base and a good deal of autonomy. They assumed that programs governed by the courts or court-related agencies would inevitably reflect the values and interests of their hosts. We will take a closer look at two community based models that were introduced in Chapter 3, Community Boards and Community Association for Mediation. I will contrast them with the Dorchester Urban Court, a community-oriented, court-sponsored model that highlights the structural implications limiting the empowerment mission.

Community Boards

When Raymond Shonholtz conceptualized the San Francisco Community Boards Program, he drew on the ideas of Nils Christie, a Scandinavian criminologist teaching on the Faculty of Law at the University of Oslo, Norway.[2] Christie viewed conflicts as valuable community properties that were being expropriated by the court system. People learn and grow by working through conflicts. To the extent that conflicts are criminalized and handled by the courts out of the neighborhood, the community becomes disempowered.

Shonholtz felt strongly that a Community Dispute Resolution program, to be truly effective, must be owned by the community it serves. He viewed "community" in geographical terms synonymous with "neighborhood". He insisted the program must be something more than just an extension of the criminal justice system or another social service agency. The goal was to encourage residents to take on the responsibility of resolving conflicts in their own neighborhoods. In order to achieve this goal, community members must learn what kinds of conflicts exist, what the causes are, what remedies are available, and how to use those remedies. That kind of knowledge becomes available when a community is fully involved in the dispute resolution process. Shonholtz proposed the Community Board Program as a means by which community members could assess and document structural problems through their experiences helping to resolve cases that were identified initially as individual conflicts.

Shonholtz was a highly effective fundraiser and was able to garner sufficient money from private sources to implement this program on a major scale. I watched with interest the development and operation of this well-funded and widely publicized program. The idea was to have community groups appoint a board or panel of people who would be trained in "conciliation".[*] Conciliation sessions were open to the public. In this neighborhood forum, four or more panelists would hear the case. In the process of helping the participants work towards agreement, the panelists could alert them to appropriate social services. The conciliators would not only help settle the community's disputes, but would also learn more about their community and its problems.

The value of having people in the neighborhood with knowledge of their community and with conciliation skills was recognized early in one Community Board neighborhood. A neighborhood organization sought to involve its citizens in planning and executing its program. They scheduled a large strategic planning meeting at which the audience would be broken down into small groups to identify relevant community problems. They turned to Community Boards mediators to facilitate these small groups. With skilled facilitators, knowledgeable about their community, the planning process moved ahead smoothly.

Community Association for Mediation (CAM)

A few small-scale attempts at developing community empowerment dispute resolution models are noteworthy. I call this model "homespun mediation". The Community Association for Mediation (CAM) in Pittsburgh attempted to build the concepts of mediation and community growth, found in the Community Board model, directly into the fabric of an African American neighborhood. Unlike most community dispute resolution project organizers, Gloria Patterson and Dorothy Williams, the originators, were active community workers in the area served by CAM, and Patterson lived there. They were also involved in most volunteer groups in their neighborhood, the Hill District, and had built a wide range of contacts. While serving on an oversight committee for my American Friends Service Committee program, Patterson learned about mediation and dispute resolution programs around the country, particularly Community Boards.

---

[*] Shonholtz used the term "conciliation" to emphasize that the process used was more open and participatory than the dominant IMCR model of mediation.

Lacking financial backing, Patterson simply identified those people in her community whom she already knew to be problem solvers: agency paraprofessionals, block club leaders, involved parents and social workers. They met informally in Patterson's home and talked about mediation. Some discovered that this fancy new label simply described what they were doing already. When they saw a need for additional training on a selected topic to enhance their skills, they designed an appropriate continuing education program around that specific topic. Concurrently, CAM notified and met with existing community leaders to inform them of the new project. Thus, they were able to avoid jurisdictional jealousy and to solicit cooperation.

This informal group decided to remain informal—as a network of residents who continued to support each other and train together. They mediated disputes that came to them primarily through their individual networks or jobs. The group met bi-weekly to discuss their experiences so they could learn from each other. In these sessions they could learn more about their community, as well as share culturally appropriate conflict resolution techniques.

The main shortcoming of this all volunteer model is that when the primary volunteer burns out or moves on, the project is likely to collapse. That is what happened. However, since the group consisted of existing community problem solvers, it can be assumed that they continued their informal troubleshooting activities on their own – with enhanced skills.

Dorchester Urban Court

The history of the Dorchester Urban Court illustrates the structural limitations of a court owned program that limit the possibility for the program to serve a community empowerment agenda. The Urban Court was developed in 1975 by the Justice Resource Institute, a nonprofit criminal justice reform agency that sought to improve the quality of justice through assisting public agencies in establishing projects such as drug rehabilitation, pretrial diversion and service delivery programs for female offenders. They located this court sponsored project in a storefront down the street from the courthouse in the Dorchester section of Boston. Dorchester is an established working class, predominately black neighborhood.

The program was designed to have a neighborhood focus within a court sponsored project. Hence it had a neighborhood advisory group and many local volunteer mediators. Despite the neighborhood focus, the project was owned tightly by the court. It received its funding, staff support, authority and most of its cases from the Municipal Court of Dorchester.

Sociologists William Felstiner and Lynne Williams conducted an extensive evaluation of the Urban Court and captured some of the subtle ways the court's control, not only of funding but of the vital resource of cases to mediate, impacted the scope of the sessions and the nature of the outcomes. For example, cases were referred from the court to mediation with paperwork labeling the parties as plaintiff and defendant, or claimant and respondent. Without having to communicate any instructions, just from filling in the papers, mediators understood that if a report of settlement was to be filed with the court, it ought to be written up as an agreement between the parties named in the complaint.

Of course community conflicts are often more complex than Party A vs. Party B. One case Felstiner and Williams observed is illustrative. It involved a complaint by a black woman that a white man had threatened her and had fired gunshots. It turns out that the woman was visiting a friend (a black man) who was present as a witness. He was having an ongoing dispute with his white neighbor that focused on the black man's dog. The mediators wrote an agreement between the complainant woman and the white man where he agreed not to threaten her in the future or discharge a weapon. The mediators were reluctant to get involved in a dispute between a named party and a third party even though he was there as a witness. If the mediators had not felt constrained to report back to the court about the "complainant" and "respondent", would they have been more likely to consider the dispute between the two neighboring men? That is where the real, ongoing dispute was. How much more difficult would it be to fit community wide issues into this format?

Tension between volunteer mediators recruited from the neighborhood and the court flared up at times. Periodic conflicts also involved the Urban Court's neighborhood advisory committee. At one point the mediators went out on strike. Later they seceded from the project and formed their own mediation program.

These periodic conflicts highlight an important issue in organizing community dispute resolution programs, especially ones with a community empowerment agenda. The lesson is that Programs tend to become molded to meet the needs of the "owner". Hence, governance or "ownership" makes a fundamental difference.

With that understanding, I strongly advocated developing CDR programs that would be independent of the courts and owned by the communities they serve. However, in retrospect I have found that it is not a matter of black and white. There are examples of community empowerment activities being conducted by programs that were controlled by the criminal justice system. For instance, 1993, after the riots arising from the videotaped beating of Rodney King by Los Angeles police, the Los Angeles City Attorney's Dispute Resolution Program undertook a series of dialogues on race relations in the city. The program's mediators were retrained and formed a core of facilitators who fanned out across the city to help open up communication and creative thinking about race relations.[3] This experience demonstrates that providing facilitators for dialogue programs, an empowering approach, is not the exclusive prerogative of community owned mediation programs.

Neighborhood Justice Centers

The tensions over the role of CDR programs and their empowerment potential was clear in the planning and development of the federal government sponsored Neighborhood Justice Centers. In 1977, Attorney General Griffin Bell, using funding he had available through LEAA (Law Enforcement Assistance Administration), established three Neighborhood Justice Centers (NJC), in Atlanta, Kansas City, and Venice (Los Angeles). They were to be experimental models to determine how federal funds could best be used to promote the expansion of community dispute resolution programs.

In 1976, I was invited to participate in the design of this experiment. I attended a planning seminar that aimed at determining what kind of programs should be included as the NJC pilot projects. I argued strongly for the inclusion of a community based model, others argued for court based models. Even though there were models of each type already in existence around the country that could use the available money and could jump start the research, the Justice

Department decided to develop three new projects. They established a community based model in Venice, a court based model in Kansas City, and a "hybrid" of the two—located in the community but with strong court sponsorship in Atlanta, Georgia.

Of these three programs, the hybrid model in Atlanta is the one that eventually was the most successful when measured on the basis of cost-effectiveness. The program used volunteer mediators from the community. Cases were referred both from the community and the courts. The Atlanta program also developed a good public training program used to generate a separate income stream.

The Venice program was touted as a grass-roots model. "Grass-roots" implied to me that at least the communities it served should govern the program. And better yet it should have a community empowerment focus.

I visited it and found it was structured in a way that did not foster community empowerment. I was convinced, in this period, that governance was a key point in analyzing the potential for empowerment. A program in which governance is within a neighborhood is likely to reflect community values. Since the Los Angeles County Bar Association appointed the board of directors, it would have been surprising if this program truly empowered community organizations. I wondered at the time whether Venice might be more accurately be called a straw man.

Even with community control of governance, there may be other parties with control of vital resources. Their needs may be different than the program's, and they will encourage the program to meet those needs before addressing the center's own priorities. An example is caseload control. It is a key to defining ownership. If most cases are referred from court, as we saw in the Dorchester example, the court's expectations will mold the program.

Conversations with various participants and observers associated with the Neighborhood Justice Center effort have convinced me that Griffin Bell saw the NJCs as an extension of court services. Even in his public comments he defined the problem as increasing access to justice rather than as returning responsibility for dispute settlement to the community.

> In many disputes, it costs too much and takes too long to go to court. We are setting up three experimental Neighborhood Justice

Centers to develop a mechanism that will provide access to justice for people who are now shut out and to provide relief to our overburdened courts by diverting matters that do not require a full court proceeding.[4]

Bell apparently did not see any role for the community in designing the Neighborhood Justice Centers, much less governing them. "The centers would be developed as pilot projects through the joint efforts of local government, the courts and the bar association".[5] A grass roots model was included in the experiment only after protests by community-oriented advocates including me. But Venice, when established, was given neither the governance structure nor the resources necessary to become a neighborhood institution.

The governance was structured from the top down resulting in the board of directors being dominated by white professionals. Although the community it served had a high concentration of low income and Mexican-Americans, they were brought in to participate only after the program had been planned. Center staff sought the support of community leaders, and some became board members. They, in turn, recommended local candidates as mediators and staff. Joel Edelman was chosen to the key position of Executive Director. He was a young attorney and did not reside in the Venice-Mar Vista area. Many of the front line staff did. The program held fiestas, participated in community organizations and demonstrated mediation through role-playing in order to increase community awareness of the center and to diversify the source of cases.

The consequences of organizing a Community based dispute resolution program governed by people from outside the community, both geographically and racially, surfaced in an interview I conducted with a staff member. I had learned that to get a solid understanding of a program I should not limit myself to talking only with the director. If I hang around the office, pitch in on volunteer tasks, or even just read, gradually some staff member or volunteer will strike up a conversation with me. This is where I get my real information about a project..

At the Venice program the staff person who struck up a conversation with me was a Mexican-American whose job description involved increasing the Mexican-American participation in the program. He observed that the NJC staff included a reasonable number of Hispanics. However, few Hispanic residents were using the center, and it was unlikely many more would participate despite the Center's recruiting activities and fiestas.

He explained that in the Mexican-American community people are reluctant to deal with conflicts face to face. They prefer to take their conflicts to someone within the community who has the respect of all parties, like a priest. The staff member went on to point out that as long as the NJC uses mediators who are not connected with the parties and have not built respect, few Mexican-Americans would come. He was frustrated that the program never considered adapting its model for processing cases to the needs of the neighborhood. If the Board had had more Hispanic neighborhood representation right from the beginning, it might have grasped that issue, and, modified the program to fit.

I raised the issue of Hispanic representation to the executive director, Joel Edelman and with the staff researcher. I was given the impression that NJC planners were reluctant to make significant changes in design of the centers or research methodologies.

The Venice program eventually was considered unsuccessful because the criteria used to evaluate the three NJCs reflected the orientation toward the courts of the Justice Department. Since the Venice grass roots model generated fewer mediations than the two NJCs that were more directly connected to courts, it looked to the evaluators like a more questionable investment. I met with Justice Department officials and wrote follow up memoranda suggesting that the evaluation criteria needed to be changed to measure the community building agenda that we had hoped for from the "community based" NJC. If criteria more related to community development had been used, the Venice program might have been rated higher. The struggles with program evaluation criteria are discussed in more depth in Chapter 6.

The experiment was supposed to guide decision making about proposed federal funding of CDR programs. In the end it did not matter which NJC won the popularity contest. The Carter administration was facing a re-election challenge by Ronald Reagan, whose major campaign issue was opposition to government spending. Carter dropped his support for the federal dispute resolution funding mechanism, the Dispute Resolution Act of 1980. Federal money for the CDR field dried up and has never been reinstated. Meanwhile the field continues to expand without federal government support.

The Battle Over Qualifications

Another area where divisiveness surfaced was over the issue of establishing qualifications for mediators. It seemed axiomatic to people earning their living from mediation, to legislators granting funds to mediation programs, and to courts that would be sending people to such programs, that there should be a clear definition of the attributes of a mediator. Typically those favoring qualification standards thought in conventional terms. For example, the original membership standards established by the Academy of Family Mediators (AFM) required an advanced degree in mental health (therapists, social workers, psychologists and psychiatrists) or law, plus 60 hours of specified training. Basically they were judging qualifications by training and degrees. These AFM membership standards were adopted in many states as standards to qualify for recognition as a mediator.

Community empowerment models tended to feel threatened by the AFM type credential/training approach. If it were applied to community mediators, most of them would find themselves barred from mediating.

Responding to the growing controversy over credentials and qualifications, in 1987 SPIDR (Society of Professionals in Dispute Resolution) convened a Commission to settle some of the more divisive questions about qualifications. George Nicolau, who was President of SPIDR, called for a broadly based Commission to examine the issues involved in writing qualifications and if possible, to develop a set of standards that would be acceptable to all factions. He selected me to serve as one of the commissioners.

The first meeting was in New York. On my way to the SPIDR meeting, I attended a meeting of the Steering Committee of the National Association for Community Justice. NACJ was an unsuccessful attempt to develop a national coordinating body for community mediators. It was dissolved around 1991.

At the NACJ meeting, I pointed out that I had been invited to join SPIDR's Commission looking into the qualifications issue and asked for their advice. Ray Shonholtz was adamant that I should not participate on the Commission. I was merely a token representative of the community mediation field. That, to him, was evidence that SPIDR was intent on imposing a narrow set of professional definitions that would ensure the survival of professional mediators and would ease out volunteer community ones.

The next morning, disregarding Shonholtz's advice, I attended the Commission meeting and relayed to the other commission members the concerns that Shonholtz and the NACJ steering committee had expressed. Immediately virtually all the Commission members spoke, emphasizing the importance of the community sector and the need to avoid curtailing its flexibility, voluntariness, and creativity.

"Now," I thought, "We are in business". And we were. What Shonholtz had overlooked was that George Nicolau was the ideal person to set up an inclusive process because he had experience in practically every sector of the conflict resolution field. He had a long career in labor relations and served as a baseball arbitrator. At the other end of the spectrum, as a Vice President of the Institute for Mediation and Conflict Resolution, he was instrumental in supporting Sandi Tamid and Ann Weisbrod when they established the IMCR Community Dispute Resolution Program.[*] The Commission members had been chosen carefully for their knowledge of the field and respect for the differences among the sectors of the field.

In the Commission's discussions we rapidly came to agreement that the needs for accountability were quite different in each sector. Labor mediators and arbitrators are generally hired by people with long experience in collective bargaining and who know the reputation of the intervenor that they hire. In contrast, divorcing couples, most likely are first time users of mediation and do not know mediators' reputations. We decided that we had to devise a structure flexible enough to fit all sectors yet concrete enough to protect consumers.

The commission evolved a few major principles.

First, qualification standards should not be established by a single body. There should be a variety of agencies working on it.

Second, no academic degree assures competence, so no degree should be used as a prerequisite for service as an intervenor.

Third, the extent to which qualifications should be mandated ought to vary by the degree of choice the parties have over who

---

[*] The IMCR Community Dispute Program is described further in Chapter 5.

is the intervenor, the dispute resolution process and the program offering the dispute resolution process. Where there is free choice on all three points, such as labor relations, all that should be required is that potential mediators provide information about themselves to help parties make decisions.

Applying the principles to the typical community dispute resolution program, the parties usually have a choice of agencies and process. They could go to court and litigate or to the CDR center and mediate. However, usually the actual mediator is assigned by program staff, and the parties have no choice. Under those circumstances, the program itself should be responsible for articulating and communicating the criteria it uses to select and oversee its mediators.

The final point, and most problematic for implementation, is that decisions as to whether one satisfies the qualifications should not be based on training, as in the AFM membership criteria. Rather the determinations should come through "performance based testing". Roughly, that means one must find a way to monitor the intervenor's skills, whether in role-plays or actual sessions.

Performance based testing seemed to be a little known and expensive process. That recommendation was the hardest one for the CR Community and those who wanted to regulate it to accept. Whether mediators are observed in role-plays, in actual cases, or in interactive video disks, considerable resources are involved. Therefore, the early AFM approach of looking at amount of training remained easier for law makers and judges to understand. One result of the commission report is that AFM dropped its requirement for a graduate degree as a prerequisite .

The full SPIDR approach to qualifications has not been adopted widely. The recognition that the qualification scheme must be tailored to the particular sector involved helped lower the tension between "professional" and "volunteer community" mediators.

We have seen that since the very first CDR programs there has been a division between court-based and community-based programs. Early writings referred to three basic models – court based, agency and community based. Although the rivalry was significant, the distinctions are becoming less important as the field matures. In the next chapters we focus primarily on community based programs and the empowerment model(s). The reader should recognize that there is a rich history of non-community based dispute resolution programming, already well documented in other works.

1. Shonholtz, Raymond, *The Citizens' Role in Justice: Building a Primary Justice and Prevention System at the Neighborhood Level*, Manuscript 1987, p. 19
2. Niles Christie, "Conflicts as Property," *The British Journal of Criminology*, Vol. 17, No. 1, January 1977, p. 1
3. Thomas, Avis R. "Dialogue: Local to National," *Conflict Resolution Notes*, Vol. 15, No. 3, 1988, p. 20
4. Griffin B. Bell, Address to Mexican-American Legal Defense Fund, February 15, 1977
5. Griffin B. Bell, Press Release, July 28, 1977

CHAPTER 5 — SPREADING THE EMPOWERMENT MODEL

The divisions between court/agency based and community empowerment based programs existed from the very beginning of the CDR movement. It was clear that the community empowerment model was fragile and needed nurturing. Given my success as a networker, I focused my energies on networking for the community-based empowerment approach to conflict resolution. I made sure that reformers could share their ideas and progress with like-minded colleagues. I assumed the role of a vocal advocate for empowerment models of CDR. I changed the name of my American Friends Service Committee project, The Pennsylvania Pretrial Justice Program, to The Grassroots Citizen Dispute Resolution Clearinghouse. Further, I renamed my quarterly periodical *The Mooter*. The title was derived from the anthropological term "moot" that describes an informal village gathering held to render justice and heal relationships.

I was able to reach a national audience using two initial approaches. The first was to distribute information through AFSC's national structure of regional offices scattered all over the country. The second was to work with and participate in national conferences. The exposure and information I received, and the contacts I made from serving on conference committees and boards of directors of national, state and local mediation associations, helped me immeasurably in building a national network of people involved in conflict resolution.

Since there were few resources available, either in the form of literature or experienced program organizers, I took on an informal consulting role in which I continually stressed empowerment issues.

Founding IMCR Community Dispute Resolution

My first, and most influential consulting effort led to the founding of the community dispute resolution program at the Institute for Mediation and Conflict Resolution (IMCR) in New York City. IMCR's community dispute resolution program was founded by two women who had worked for the New York City Court Pre-Trial Diversion Program. In their previous positions, Ann Weisbrod and Sandi Tamid had circulated a form letter saying they were very dissatisfied with pre-trial diversion and asked respondents for more effective ideas for criminal justice reform. I had just written some articles about the Community Assistance Program in Chester, and the 4A program in Rochester, and in response to the form letter, I sent these articles with an invitation to call me for further information.

Soon, I received a telephone call from Weisbrod, telling me that she and Tamid had quit their jobs to organize a community mediation program—IMCR—and were working closely with the police department in New York City to support a precinct-wide program. The police were very cooperative in planning and developing the IMCR Community Dispute Program because they saw these disputes as essentially, family or neighbor problems that they viewed as mainly social work cases rather than real criminal cases.

IMCR became very influential because it developed one of the first training programs for volunteer mediators. More importantly, IMCR trained mediation staff and volunteer mediators throughout the Northeast. The "IMCR Model" became the standard training model that prevailed for many years.

North Carolina

One of my most memorable and extensive consulting experiences from this period was my connection with Charlotte Adams, of Chapel Hill, North Carolina. This intervention illustrates some of the complexities of establishing a truly community empowering CDR program.

Adams was the wife of a retired University of North Carolina professor. She held a peace vigil every Wednesday outside the courthouse in Chapel Hill for years during the Vietnam War. She eventually became a court watcher—she would sit in the courtroom taking notes, and at the end of the session she would lecture the judge about how he could handle disputes better.

Somehow Adams heard about my work. She wrote saying she wanted to start a mediation center in Chapel Hill. She requested materials that would help her accomplish this goal. Her inquiry initiated a series of phone calls between us, and eventually she asked me to train the group she had assembled. I declined because I did not view myself as a trainer. In fact, at that stage, I had not been trained either. I had purposely avoided being trained, while I actively sought out information about the various training models that were emerging. I wanted to have a good understanding of the broad training field without feeling locked into one style. It was not until 1980 that I took my first mediation training.

I did agree to come to Chapel Hill to consult with Adams and her group about establishing a community based dispute resolution center.

When I arrived, she put me up in a little garage apartment behind her house. She informed me that she had formed a committee that was expecting me to train them to mediate between 5 and 7 PM for the next three days. Charlotte Adams was not one to let go of an idea easily! I suggested using the time to think through how best to achieve their goals. (I was stubborn too.) They needed to work on some difficult issues if their goal was to establish an empowering community change oriented dispute resolution program. For instance, the committee was an all-white group composed mainly of the University of North Carolina retired faculty and their spouses. They had the active support of both the current District Attorney and his challenger in an upcoming election. However, the community likely to be served by this project, which was less educated and had significant African American representation, was not involved in planning the project.

In the three days I used for planning we worked through ways to increase diversity and to obtain free training. The Chapel Hill program did broaden in diversity during the three days I was there and continued work in this area after I left. However it was still heavily influenced by white faculty.

My three day consulting effort seemed to have worked even though, at this stage, not only had I no mediation training, I had never organized a CDR program. I had only read all that was available and garnered ideas at conferences. But few people had more information or experience.

The program eventually moved to the neighboring township, Carrboro, and became the Orange County Dispute Settlement Center, where it draws from a more diverse population.

The Chapel Hill group, at my suggestion, managed to obtain training from the Southeast Regional Office of Community Relations Service (CRS), a federal agency that specialized in mediating in civil rights situations. I knew they had done the first round of training for Community Boards in San Francisco. Several of the early community mediation projects took advantage of the availability of free training offered by this program, but soon CRS stopped providing it.

This Orange County Dispute Settlement Program initially operated as a low-budget, volunteer-run, community model conflict resolution program. The director, Scott Bradley, was a restaurant manager who could monitor the telephone answering machine. Eventually, they obtained funding from two sources: (1) discretionary money allocated by the North Carolina legislature for each legislator to spend on behalf of constituents called "walking around money", and (2) Interest on Law Office Trust Accounts (IOLTA) which consists of money held in trust for attorneys' clients. Attorneys' ethics forbid them from profiting from their clients' funds that they may be holding. IOLTA plans provide a way to pool these funds and apply the interest accrued to charities. The support that the program had developed came in handy when they filed an application with the Bar Association for IOLTA funding.

Charlotte Adams' successes were important steps in spreading the idea of mediation and the availability of funding for mediation programs around North Carolina. Today, every major city in the state has a mediation program. Most of these programs are court-based rather than community-based. Eventually these North Carolina programs formed a state association and managed to get regular state funds appropriated for mediation centers.

New York State: Building State Support for Community Empowerment Projects

Another early statewide program originally began as an initiative of little mediation programs centered in the Upstate New York areas: Schenectady, Albany, Batavia, and Troy. These programs tended to be Quaker influenced and involved community-based models. Some of them were housed in Quaker meeting houses. Some were trained by Friends Suburban Project. I visited these programs in 1979 and observed that, although some of the organizers were interested in community empowerment, and all wanted to involve the black community, the programs had not been able to include many African Americans, either as mediators, or as participants. Also, these programs were terribly underfunded and were having a very hard time getting cases.

These New York mediation programs came together and agreed that it would be helpful to establish a state-funded office to support community dispute resolution. In March 1979 I learned of the pending legislation from Lou Fiscarelli, director of the Albany Dispute Mediation Program. At his suggestion, I wrote to the Nassau Coalition for Safety and Justice, a community based criminal justice organization with strong church support, to suggest kicking off their campaign with a conference.

> Senator Ornstein's office is on the verge, I am told, of putting a good sounding bill into the hopper that would provide NY State funding to community based mediation programs ... Seems to me it might be useful if you are interested, to pull together some sort of statewide meeting after the bill has been put in. It could perform a dual function. Primary role would be to lay a base for lobbying in support of the bill. Secondary function would be to get the various mediation folk together, and like minded souls, to talk shop. [1]

The Nassau Coalition referred me to the Community Justice Institute, which agreed to co-sponsor a statewide conference to promote legislation for a state office. We invited all the New York State mediation programs to a conference in Albany to describe their programs and report on their funding and other program needs. Eighty participants, from five states, attended it. The experience base was so narrow that if we had limited it to New York programs there would have been little information to share. Most of the New York programs were just starting up. However, the conference served as an important step in the campaign to enact the Ornstein bill. It is likely that this conference was the first in the country exclusively focusing on community conflict resolution.

The mediation programs in New York were successful in passing the legislation that established a state office, in 1981. There were several reasons for their success. First, they took action in a period when funding was plentiful. LEAA funds were still being allocated to states to improve the criminal justice system. Second, significant groups with a statewide scope backed the concept. One was the Junior League, which counted among its membership the wives of influential men within the state (influential women were rare in business and politics in 1979). Third, the Community Justice Institute also had a statewide presence and could mobilize a large constituency of people concerned with reforming the criminal justice system.

Organizing also may have been facilitated by the fact that cities in Upstate New York were linked together by a good train system. It was relatively easy for mediation program staff to travel, visit, and support each other.

As a result, New York became the first state with a state funding mechanism for mediation programs. Community-based models were favored since the groups lobbying for funds were mostly independent non-profit organizations. Funding was granted only to programs run by independent non-profit organizations, not directly to the courts.

One would think that community empowered models would thrive under this funding arrangement. However, two trends developed. The courts discovered ways to arrange for non-profit fronts, such as the Bar Association, through which programs could be funded. Second, since the state office granting the money was housed in the State Court Administrative Office, the statistics required from the programs to assure the funds were being well-used, were highly court oriented. The programs reported caseloads and cost effectiveness figures. Just as was required of the Neighborhood Justice Centers. These criteria tended to pull groups away from broad-based community empowerment ideals and toward individual case management processes. I will examine this phenomenon more closely in the next chapter.

In spite of the structure shifting programs away from community empowerment, a careful reading of the New York State Community Dispute Resolution Program's annual report[2] indicates that some CDR centers continued to serve as a community resource.

This information shows up in the individual program listings under the heading "Additional Program Information". While the data sheets directly ask for information about "Referrals and Involvement in Courts", referrals and involvement in the community apparently fall under a category equivalent to "other".

The "Additional " information indicates that the Ulster-Sullivan Mediation program has provided election monitors for non-profit organizations. Washington Heights Innwood Coalition Mediation Project operates a housing program, a parent support group and other programs. Community empowerment is not dead in New York, but it is relegated to the status of "Additional Information".

A Matter of Definition

The New York experience mirrors national trends in a second manner: it muddies program definitions. From the very beginning of the community dispute resolution movement I identified three basic models: court, agency, and community governed programs. I wrote extensively using that typology and argued strongly that only the community governed program has the real potential for strengthening and empowering communities. This typology came to be used frequently in the literature.

However, over time the distinctions between "agency" and "community" run programs lost any meaning. In the 1970s, there was a fairly clear distinction between a community and neighborhood run program, such as the Community Association for Mediation, and an agency program, such as the Rochester 4A program. The 4A program was centralized, took cases from any part of the city and was responsible to a city-wide board of directors. Community Association for Mediation operated in one neighborhood only, was governed by neighbors, and did its work in the neighborhood.

Community based programs (as detailed in Chapter 6) tended to grow and expand their services to larger and larger geographical areas. Their governing structures reflected the expansion; they were no longer controlled by or responsible to the interests of any particular neighborhood. This trend is detailed in the next chapter.

Meanwhile, agency programs tended to decentralize and hold sessions in the neighborhoods where disputes arose and to draw on volunteer mediators, similar to those used by community based programs.

The agency/community concept became a meaningless distinction and dropped out of use. Current usage only distinguishes court programs and community ones. The National Association for Community Mediation (NACFM) uses a lengthy definition.

Community (or Community based) programs can be "characterized by, and/or committed to: (1) the use of trained community volunteers as the primary providers of mediation services; volunteers are not required to have academic or professional credentials; (2) a private non-profit or public agency, or program thereof, with a governing/advisory board; (3) mediators, staff and governing/advisory board are representative of the diversity of the community served; (4) providing direct access of mediation to the public through self referral and striving to reduce barriers to service including physical, linguistic, cultural, programmatic and economic; (5) providing service to clients regardless of their ability to pay; (6) initiating, facilitating and educating for collaborative community relationships to effect positive systemic change; (7) engaging in public awareness and educational activities about the values and practices of mediation; (8) providing a forum for dispute resolution at the early stages of the conflict; and (9) providing an alternative to the judicial system at any stage of the conflict.[3]

Programs that do not fit most of the criteria above are designated as court based. This simplified typology will be used in the rest of this book.

In the thirteen years from 1973–1980 CDR evolved from a germ of an idea to a movement. A variety of projects developed with an eye on community empowerment. Many were pulled together with shoe-string budgets while federal funds went primarily to their own experimental models – the Neighborhood Justice Centers. Early organizers struggled to locate funding sources, and develop appropriate training models. State funded resource networks began to be created and national associations began to evolve. As we shall see in the next chapter, there were many impediments to the empowerment approach.

1. Paul Wahrhaftig, letter to Nassau Coalition for Safety and Justice
2. New York State Unified Court System, Office of Alternative Dispute Resolution Programs, *Community Dispute Resolution Centers Program 2000-2002 Annual Report*
3. National Association for Community Mediation, http://www.nafcm.org/pg5.cfm, as of June 12, 2003

CHAPTER 6 — IMPEDIMENTS

When I was a boy, my parents took me up north on the Pacific Coast, where we saw fish ladders built to help the salmon get past the dams on their way upstream to spawn. They would jump from one water-box to another – often missing the box and falling to die gasping on the ground below. Yet somehow many succeeded in reaching the top where they could swim on until they met the next obstacle. This image applies to empowerment-model CDR programs. So many forces and structural impediments create barriers that stand in the way of implementing the empowerment vision. As a result, many programs have flopped over and died, while others have surmounted the obstacles and carried on with their mission. In this chapter, I take a closer look at barriers to success.

Research and Evaluation

I have already alluded to a common problem highlighted by the experience of the Neighborhood Justice Centers (NJCs) and the New York state programs: inappropriate evaluation tends to distort programs away from community empowerment and towards streamlining the judicial system's service delivery. A closer look at the NJC, New York, and other programs' research component is instructive.

When the federal government funded Neighborhood Justice Centers in Kansas City, Atlanta, and Venice, they included a strong research component. They sought to compare the effectiveness of the three models (Court based, "hybrid", and community, respectively). The researchers collected comparable data from all three programs. They looked at the number of cases, types of cases, settlement rates,

participant satisfaction, and the extent to which people complied with
their agreements.[1]

While these criteria were quite relevant to the courts, they had
little to do with any sort of community empowerment goals. The result
is that public officials looked at the Atlanta and Kansas City projects
as the most effective models and the Venice community model was
viewed as the weak sister. Would the impression have been different
if the evaluation team had gathered information indicating to what
extent individuals and/or groups had become more involved in civic
development than they were before the program existed?

New York

This problem of evaluations based on the wrong criteria consistently
has plagued the empowering model. As we saw, the New York State
office, The Community Dispute Resolution Program is housed in the
Court Administrator's office. It was founded with major effort and
input from the emerging community mediation programs. At the 1979
North Eastern Regional Conflict Resolution Workshop conference in
Albany, New York, which I helped organize to kick off the campaign
for a New York state office, many of the mediation programs were
exploring empowerment issues and were trying to avoid being
dominated by the courts. For instance, they looked to recruiting cases
from sources within the community rather than having them assigned
from the courts. That approach to case development should not only
provide an excellent service for the disputants, but it should strengthen
the reputation of the community person or agency that referred the
dispute to mediation. Such a reputation for knowing where and how
to refer people is an important element of empowerment.

It had seemed to be a positive development, when funding
for New York conflict resolution programs became available
from a state fund and grants could not be paid directly to courts.
Recipients had to be non-profit organizations. However, as with the
Neighborhood Justice Centers, all state funded mediation programs
had to submit standardized data. All of the questions focused
on caseload, type of cases, how completed, and satisfaction rates.

This narrow approach discouraged local programs from becoming
involved in community empowerment work. For example, pressure
to increase the number of cases causes the programs to focus on

developing caseload from court referrals. It is much more efficient to work with a couple of court officials who can release dozens of cases than to meet with dozens of community organizations that may refer one or two cases a year. The New York data gathering system created just this sort of pressure. The programs needed to keep up their numbers of cases handled, disputes diverted from court, and satisfied participants to justify receiving government funds.

Why this Disjuncture?

Why did this disjuncture develop? Why were empowerment programs evaluated on criteria unrelated to their goals? One answer is the economics of research. It is much easier, less time consuming, and thus less expensive to count case folders and send satisfaction surveys to participants, than to measure a program's impact on a whole community. To identify the extent that anyone has become more able to influence the forces that control them, requires new study designs, extensive interviewing and gathering of qualitative data. This is a very labor-intensive proposition.

Another explanation might be called the Con Job Consequence. Funding for community dispute resolution has never been plentiful; even less so for empowerment models. Organizers and advocates of community empowerment dispute resolution programs were building on the community organizing experiments of the 1960s. In a 1977 article spelling out the philosophy behind organizing such programs I wrote, "Empowerment must be understood in its political context, ordinarily this means power exercised by people working together in groups".[2] However, community empowerment was no longer a priority for most funding sources.

The funders had a different agenda than the CDR empowerment organizers. In the 1970s LEAA's focus was on fighting crime by streamlining law enforcement and making it more effective. In the 1980s funders were concentrating on substance abuse, and in the 1990s on violence. Community dispute resolution programs frequently wrote their descriptions and grant proposals in terms designed to meet the funders' goals. They would claim in a proposal to LEAA, for instance, that the mediation project would reduce court overload. In the 1980s, they would hint that if families mediated their problems, drug and alcohol abuse might be reduced. And in the 1990s, mediation projects, particularly in schools, promised reductions in violence.

Having conned the funders by promising to reduce caseloads, ameliorate substance abuse, or prevent violence, programs could not complain when they were asked to submit data showing they had accomplished what they had promised.

There were the exceptions; programs that were clear and articulate about their real goals and motives. San Francisco's Community Boards is a leading example. Raymond Shonholtz, its first Executive Director, managed to resist any evaluation based on traditional case statistics. He insisted that good research should speak to the goal of empowerment. This insistence led to a good deal of ferment in the academic community over attempts to develop a research model that would fit. Two leaders in this effort were Fred DuBow, who got the contract to study Community Boards, and Sally Merry, who helped bring DuBow's findings to publication after his untimely death.

DuBow's analysis of what questions to ask is still relevant for community empowerment programs to avoid competing on efficiency measures, like case management issues. Here are some measures he used at Community Boards in 1985.

> We need to look at impact – what difference does [the program] make? [First] there are **disputes**. What will we be able to say about the disputes that came to the program? Why did they settle? How did the program alter the conflicts?
>
> **Disputants:** You can … have no effect on the conflict but still affect the people. For example – a conflict that wasn't completely resolved but the parties learned a lot about settling future conflicts.
>
> **Volunteers:** What difference does this program make to volunteers? Does it change them? Have their skills or community involvement changed?
>
> **Community:** What impact on the community? Is the neighborhood different for having a community-based program in it?
>
> [DuBow listed sources of information for the four impact areas and then cautioned,] Even if you found some results, the question is, "Why did it happen?" You need to know not only what the program said it was going to do, but what did it actually do.

Costs: Every program is accountable about costs and benefits. CR programs are getting a bum rap in most evaluation cost studies. Court cost studies are terrible. I have never seen a calculation of a court case that includes lawyers' training, yet we include all the training costs when we look at CR programs.[3]

Other Impediments

Other unique challenges and pressures have pushed many community empowerment type programs into becoming totally focused on service delivery. These impediments act in concert with the research problems to discourage a community empowerment orientation. It is no surprise that these programs are a minority in the field and are marginally funded.

Community empowerment dispute resolution programs and court programs may look similar. They may use volunteer mediators, have an office outside the courthouse, and receive some of their cases from outside the court system. However, their goals are markedly different. Typically, court based programs are there to reduce court congestion, and save taxpayers money while rendering mediation services.

Community empowerment programs are trying to help people, particularly poor people and minorities, to increase their influence over the institutions and forces that shape their lives. They have little real interest in reducing court congestion.

The contrast is well illustrated by the Community Youth Mediation Program in Cleveland, Ohio. It ran a highly effective youth mediation program that dealt with individual truancy cases and, using information developed from those experiences, successfully advocated for change in the truancy system. However, since CYMP was neighborhood based, it did not reach other parts of the city or their schools. So the courts, building on the pioneering work done by the community based program, established mediation programs in the rest of the schools in Cleveland. While the new court programs may have handled the individual disputes well, reducing the load on juvenile court; the advocacy and community education functions were missing, as were the programs themselves once outside funding dried up.

The CYMP example illustrates the premise that programs serve the interests of their owners. Similar school conflict resolution programs within the same school system achieved different goals depending on whether the program was established by CYMP or the courts.

Impediment: Geographical Scope

Most empowerment oriented CDR programs initially were organized on a neighborhood level with a goal of enhancing the self-sufficiency of the neighborhood. Over the years they grew to cover larger and larger geographical areas, quickly they passed the point where their constituency was small enough that community empowerment activities were possible, or sensible.

As programs are pressured to handle more cases to justify their expenses, they tend to turn to the police, minor courts, or trial courts to send them their cases. Each of these sources has its own definition of its jurisdiction or constituency. Further, courts and police usually perceive that they are under a constitutional mandate to treat everyone in their jurisdictions equally. Thus, when a CDR program moves from only handling walk-ins from the neighborhood to getting referrals from the police, staff will find themselves handling cases from the entire precinct. If they tap into the trial level court they will receive cases from everywhere in the county. This is the beginning of the process by which a reform program gradually comes to mimic the institution it was supposed to reform.

Such changes had an impact on the development of the IMCR Community Dispute Resolution program in New York City, even though the program was never designed to empower the community. The IMCR program was established to provide a more humane city service, according to George Nicolau, its Vice President. [4] However, the same jurisdictional pressures led to major changes.

The program opened in a converted brownstone in Harlem. I visited it soon afterwards, early in 1975, and observed:

> A story best illustrates the difference between this community mediation program and the traditional criminal justice system. Sandi Tamid came home from working her 1 to 9 plus PM shift at the center greatly wrought up. An attempt at mediation of a crucial case had not worked and she felt that one of the reasons was that the atmosphere for the parties was not quite right. Waiting areas are too congested. There is a lot of chaotic movement of mediators, staff and parties in and out of rooms, up and down stairs, and in general the parties were not made to feel properly at ease. [During a sleepless night she developed a solution] which involved moving her office upstairs, which would require her to climb more stairs per day than she would have liked. [5]

By the late 1970s, when I visited again, the project had received full city funding and had moved to a former charity hospital. Now clients waited in dim halls, sitting on institutional plastic chairs, until they were called to their sterile hearing room. I could detect a trend towards shorter hearings and more willingness to resort to arbitration to move the mass of cases the project had to deal with. In 1978, the IMCR center handled 2225 cases, of which all but 336 were referred by a criminal justice agency. The cases came from everywhere in Manhattan, and the center extended its jurisdiction to the entire city of New York in June 1979.[6]

The difference can be attributed to the fact that IMCR was successful in obtaining full funding from the mayor's office. Since a mayor's constituency is the whole city, he is unlikely to maintain a project that works only in one portion of the city. Thus, program changes needed to be made to accommodate the wider jurisdiction and the increased number of participants. Each step took IMCR farther from any manageable neighborhood or community base.

Impediment: Funding/Training

In 1981, I was involved in another situation in which the disjuncture between the program's goals and the funder's vision set the program back significantly. I was acting as an advisor to Deidre Levdansky, who was organizing the Stanton Heights Community Mediation Program. Later, this project was renamed the Pittsburgh Mediation Center and still thrives today. Our goal was to build a community-based mediation program. We wanted the mediators' training to be consistent with our objective. I knew that Community Boards Program had contracted with the Community Relations Service (CRS) for its first round of training. CRS, the arm of the US Justice Department that mediated civil rights situations, conducted a good quality training, but it did not quite fit Community Boards' needs. The program ended up modifying the CRS training model and tailoring it to fit their objectives. Then they retrained staff and volunteers.

We wanted to avoid that problem, so we chose as our trainers Dorothy Williams and Gloria Patterson of the very "homespun" Community Association for Mediation (CAM) program in Pittsburgh. However, our main funder, The Pittsburgh Foundation, strongly suggested that we ought to contract with an experienced trainer with a solid reputation in the field, not some local community people with no credentials.

Taking the hint, we contracted with Ernie Odom of the Suffolk County (Coram) NY mediation program, the mixed results are described in Chapter 3.

There was and still is no cookie cutter model for organizing a community-based conflict resolution program. Each step needs to be defined carefully using the question: what impact does this approach have on the program's goals?

Impediment: Housing

An important organizing decision is where to house the program. From the very earliest community mediation programs, it was clear that such programs must be located physically outside of the courthouse if they are to be seen as independent from the court. But where to put them? A community organization, such as the Stanton Heights Civic Association, in Pittsburgh, certainly provides a convenient base in the neighborhood and is likely to have a common interest in community organizing and empowerment. However, there are two major drawbacks. First, if the civic organization is functioning well, it probably has taken a stand on controversial neighborhood issues-such as development. If so, already it has friends and enemies and consequently may not be perceived to be impartial or fair.

Secondly, most civic associations are poorly funded and lurch from one fiscal crisis to the next. Unless the civic association sees the CR program as at the core of the association's work, the mediation program is likely to be cut when the first crisis looms. This sort of partnership with civic associations has failed frequently over the years.

However, there are examples of excellent community conflict resolution programs housed in community centers. Rather than originating from outside the agency and seeking a partnering relationship, these CR programs were developed by the community center with involvement at the top level. The Cleveland Mediation Center, St. Stephens Community House in Toronto and the Good Shepherd Program in Philadelphia are three excellent programs run out of activist community centers. From the beginning they were built into the center's priorities as a valuable community resource.

Many of the early programs were housed in a church or Friends Meeting House or used neighborhood churches as satellite centers for mediation sessions. Advantages to this arrangement are clear. It is economical because programs were seldom charged rent. Buildings were secure and usually at good accessible locations. Churches are likely to share the program's community-building values. But there are drawbacks. A church setting may be problematic for a person of another religion or denomination or one who is alienated from religion. And what happens if one party is a member of the sponsoring denomination and the other is not? Will the forum be perceived as fair? Most community mediation programs that were housed in churches moved to independent quarters as soon as they could afford to do so. Church housing was an excellent stepping-stone towards implementing the program, but was not a permanent home.

The Pittsburgh Mediation Center developed a more innovative approach. It entered a partnering relationship with the Carnegie Library System in Pittsburgh PA. Under this arrangement, the public library gave the program office space in one library and access to conference rooms in all branch libraries for mediation sessions. The library willingly paid one half of a staff coordinator's salary. The library's agenda was simple. They wanted to be viewed not just as a source of books, but as an information provider to the public. That goal certainly was not inconsistent with PMC's goals.

The PMC gained neutral sites in every neighborhood, as few people have been alienated by their library. The library's funding is fairly stable and has an interest in the center's success since it brings more potential users into the library. That arrangement lasted ten years, until the center outgrew its administrative office space and moved to quarters of its own. It still uses branch libraries for the actual mediation sessions.

Conclusion

A decade after I had first seen salmon jumping up fish ladders, I was backpacking though the Sierras. At about 10,000 feet elevation I came across a stream alive with hundreds of ragged, bruised, salmon laying their eggs as they were about to expire. Their persistence in swimming upstream to that altitude, overcoming all the obstacles along the way, assured the continuation of the species. It was a wondrous sight. It is equally amazing that so many change oriented CDR programs have coped with and survived the many obstacles that pressure programs to turn away from their vision. Perseverance of this kind will assure continuation of CDR as a social movement. More challenges await as we will discuss in the next chapter. Confronting racism and other–isms within your own organization as well as society is a major task.

1. See Royer F. Cook, Janice A. Roehl, and David I. Sheppard, *Neighborhood Justice Centers Field Test: Final Evaluation Report – Executive Summary*, US Dept. of Justice, National Institute of Justice, 1980

2. Paul Wahrhaftig, "Empowerment of Communities: A Philosophy Behind CDR Organizing," *The Mooter* Vol. 1, No. 1, 1977, p. 15

3. As excerpted and reprinted in "Evaluating Community Based Conflict Resolution Programs" by Fred DuBow *Conflict Resolution Notes*, Vol. 2, No. 3, 1985, p. 25

4. Paul Wahrhaftig, "An Overview of Community-Oriented Citizen Dispute Resolution Programs in the United States", *The Politics of Informal Justice*, Vol. 1, Richard L. Abel, ed., Academic Press, 1982, p. 75, 79

5. Paul Wahrhaftig, "Community Dispute Center New York – Some Observations," *The Citizen Dispute Organizer's Handbook*, Paul Wahrhaftig, Ed., American Friends Service Committee, 1981, p. 33

6. *Community Dispute Resolution Centers Program, First Annual Report*, New York State Unified Court System, 1979

CHAPTER 7 — EXCLUSION TO DIVERSITY

It seems ironic that the early proponents of community mediation in this country focused on providing a mechanism for empowerment of blacks and minorities. The irony is that the early programs and organizations providing mediation services were designed, staffed and administered mainly by people with white middle-class experiences and values. It became clear quickly that the black community and other minority groups simply did not want to be served by these programs and became removed, neither using nor participating to any great extent. A mismatch had been set up between the goals of the providers and the needs and desires of the communities to be served.

This situation occurred not because of a lack of trying, but more from a lack of awareness of why targeted groups felt left out. The story of the community conflict resolution movement's struggle to become an ethnically and culturally diverse field is a study in overcoming institutional racism. This term applies to the structure and culture of an institution that excludes people regardless of the intent of members of the dominant culture who run the organization. The result is that minorities continue to be disempowered by the very organizations that seek to empower them. We will see how this struggle played out both at the community level and with national organizations.

The difficulties were apparent in the early days of organizing some of the upstate New York programs. The community dispute resolution programs I had contact with generally were organized by college educated white women who lived outside the community being served and were often either Quakers or Jews. They tended not to have the ability or resources to reach directly into the communities they wanted to serve. Rather they approached "the community" through agency heads whom they could talk to easily. The agency heads, in turn, often were middle-class whites also and had difficulty reaching out to people living in the neighborhood. Faced with these obstacles, the organizers followed their natural leads and recruited like-minded people as volunteers and mediators. The result was well-intentioned programs that excluded real participation by people of color.

Dan Joyce, Director of the Cleveland Mediation Center, provides an illustration of the problems community conflict resolution programs have faced in overcoming institutional racism. He recalled an early attempt to boost participation of Latin Americans from the neighborhood. The staff recruited and trained Latin American mediators, but discovered that they still were not getting any cases from that community. On further inquiry, they learned that the newly trained mediators were quite busy mediating cases outside the center around the neighborhood.

Why were these cases being mediated in the neighborhood rather than the center? With a little research CMP concluded that the Latin American community perceived the center to be another bureaucracy. Many neighborhood residents were immigrants who were fearful of deportation, even if they were in the country legally. Also, the mediation center was viewed with mistrust partially because it kept records that might come to the attention of immigration officials. It is better to remain invisible than to make yourself known to an organization that might report you to the authorities.[1]

Another example of the thinking of the early 1980s was NCPCR (National Conference on Peacemaking and Conflict Resolution). It held its first conference in Athens, Georgia in 1983. Its bi-annual conferences welcomed and embraced community mediators. It became a key forum for mediators to discuss experiences and ideas. For nearly two decades NCPCR served as a gauge of conflict resolution thinking, as well as a platform for influencing the field by surfacing new directions and connecting people from all over the world.

In the early 1980s, most of the NCPCR organizers and participants did not recognize the mismatch between the white middle class model of community mediation services and the minorities they intended to serve.

I raised the issue at the very first NCPCR, in 1983. I was on a panel on *Building Networks of Conflict Resolution Programs*. I began my presentation with, "I have a fear that conflict resolution programs and service networks reflect the collegial and peer networks of the organizers more than the substantive needs".[2] Referring to the New York example, I predicted the same unconscious exclusion would happen in NCPCR, that was happening in local programs and in my own networking activities. The consequences of the lack of meaningful minority participation in my work were apparent in the product. For example, in 1980 I published an index to four volumes of my quarterly periodical *The Mooter.* That index had no topic heading for "diversity", "cross cultural", or any other multi-ethnic category.

Understanding racial and ethnic diversity issues involved a slow learning process for many of us in the dominant society. I first began to wrestle with these issues, in the context of CDR programs, when I viewed a landlord-tenant mediation in the San Francisco Bay region. The landlord was Euro-American, the tenant was Chinese-American. The tenant was very urbane, worked for a bank, wore a nicely tailored three-piece pin striped suit and appeared to be fully assimilated. During the mediation the tenant kept shying away from pressing for his interests. The mediator kept pushing the tenant to assert himself. Finally, the parties agreed it was time to take a break. The mediator left the room. The parties settled the case quickly before the mediator returned. The settlement meant that the tenant would have to vacate. Afterwards I asked him whether the settlement worked for him. He said, "No, but I am not a confrontational person". The mediator never realized that face to face confrontational tactics were inconsistent with the tenant's culture.

Cultural diversity began to surface as an issue in San Francisco as early as 1977. The 4A program (Arbitration as an Alternative) was administered by the American Arbitration Association with close ties to the District Attorney's office. It was ahead of its time in defining issues and developing information about cultural diversity in the field.

In 1978, I wrote the only contemporary published article I know of about this experiment.

> Last year 4A began receiving some feedback that their process was irrelevant to some of San Francisco's minority communities. 4A staff, realizing that they might be facing some important cross-cultural problems responded well. They invited in representatives from some of the minority communities that had been raising

questions to analyze 4A. The resulting information would help define whether the program was useful to their communities or how it could be modified to better serve different neighborhoods. The openness of 4A's staff in programming critical analysis of their project is a very healthy sign.

The workshop, held last fall, was attended by Anglos, Latinos, Blacks, Chinese and Japanese. They went through the 4A training program for two days and then spent a day raising questions and suggesting changes. Here are some, but by no means all of, the problems they raised.

Problems

1. In many communities there is a hesitancy about involving "outsiders" in resolving disputes. Japanese and Chinese communities were specifically cited as ones in which disputes are generally resolved by the family. Thus, instead of using the traditional "neutral" who is a stranger to the parties involved, it would be necessary to pick "neutrals" who are known to the parties and recognized as responsible and trustworthy.

2. It was repeatedly pointed out that at least one of the neutrals should come from the communities in which the parties live who is familiar with the context of the dispute. Someone of the same race but from across town is just not the same as people who live in the community. In some communities, because they are small and tightly knit, it would be almost impossible to select a neutral that does not know the disputants. Thus, if 4A were to localize its neutrals, they would inevitably have to confront problem number 1.

3. The 4A format is limited to interpersonal individual conflicts-- usually between two individuals. There are other conflicts where 4A services were seen as valuable. Conflicts between the community and government agencies were cited specifically. 4A's impressive downtown office site was seen as an intimidating place to hold hearings. The process should go to the community rather than require the community to come to 4A's turf. The criticism even went to the square tables around which parties sat. Round hearing tables were seen as less intimidating.

4. The process was seen as too adversarial and conducive to hard line positions. Unfortunately, the memo was not very specific on this issue.

5. Pamphlets and literature, even the Chinese translations, are not very readable.

6. In some communities there are already existing dispute resolution processes. Japanese communities were cited as having existing mechanisms. There might be a need for 4A however. It was suggested that if at intake the disputing parties decide not to use the 4A process as is, the program should seek to find why the process was not used and what they would prefer as a dispute resolution process.

7. The nature of the arbitration, which is described in the submission to arbitration agreement signed by all parties, is that the arbitrator's final decision is unchangeable This structure is too similar to Immigration Department processes for some people.

8. Some societies are much more non-verbal, especially when personal feelings are involved.

9. Written submission forms and written agreements at the end of the hearing make some people who are not literate uncomfortable. How about using agreements dictated onto tape in those cases?

10. Policy of not paying neutrals any stipend was seen as discriminatory particularly against single parents.[3]

This study was never presented publicly or disseminated other than in this article. I think the 4A staff felt the information gathered was too threatening to distribute. To comply with its recommendations would require the dominant culture organization to make major adjustments to accommodate other cultures.

The 1984 National Conference on Peacemaking and Conflict Resolution in St. Louis provided another opportunity to take the pulse of the conflict resolution field. I experienced a reticence to examine cultural impacts on mediation similar to the attitude I had encountered at the first conference in Athens.

I was on a major panel in which, once again, I referred to my findings from visiting New York State community mediation programs. The vast majority of mediators in these programs were college-educated white women. All of my fellow panelists were white males; a fact that I did not hesitate to point out. The resulting heated discussion marked the first time that diversity issues had been raised publicly on a major platform at NCPCR.

Newham Conflict and Change Program

Consistent with my growing interest in understanding the way different cultures handled conflict, I was able to bring two participants to the conference from London, England. They were Jonathan Gosling and Janaki Mahendran from the Newham Conflict and Change Program in the East End of London. That was an area comprised of Cockney working class whites, Afro-Caribbeans and Asians. Mahendran was a refugee from Sri Lanka. Gosling's background was with the Tavistock Institute, an organization that had developed a therapeutic group process in which people from diverse backgrounds were brought together in unstructured groups. Learning came from participating in the work of the group and simultaneously examining the group dynamics. These socially diverse groups were then studied to understand how the members related to and learned from each other.

At the conference, Gosling and Mahendran described the Newham program that had grown out of this group process. The fundamental shape of their conflict resolution program was developed through a series of group retreats with full multi-ethnic participation. This model appeared highly relevant in addressing the cultural diversity issues of community mediation in that setting. For example, their approach did not require people to sit down to face-to-face mediations at a community mediation facility. Rather, staff members were likely to visit parties in their homes and relay messages back and forth. Cultural norms were recognized and woven directly into the structure of the dispute resolution process. Gosling and Mahendran's presentation was an eye opener for American CDR workers as they began to discuss "cross-cultural" approaches to conflict resolution.

By the 1986 NCPCR conference in Denver, cross-cultural issues in mediation had become a legitimate topic. This conference marked a change in the discourse from whether there were cultural differences to what the differences were. I believe that there were two primary reasons for this emerging awareness. In order to address the challenge of cultural differences, I had invited Peter McLachlan, the director of the Belfast Voluntary Welfare Society in Northern Ireland, to speak about his experiences negotiating cease-fire agreements. He gave a stimulating plenary talk about cultural differences in Northern Ireland. Sometimes it is easier to see cultural issues when you examine another society. It becomes possible, then, to apply that insight at home.

Many of his observations about cultural differences between Irish Catholics (whom he referred to as "I culture") and Protestant Unionists (referred to as "U culture") proved applicable to several other cultural clashes. For example:

> Finally, there are important cognitive differences in the cultures. The "I" culture draws on its Thomist theology when framing ideas. They have a broad framework, sometimes quite rigid, inside which there is flexibility. By contrast, the "U" culture draws on the 95 Theses of Luther and the 39 Articles of the Anglican tradition and develops ideas, proposition by proposition, working on each agenda item and not concerned about any overall framework.
>
> The 'I' culture always says to the "U culture - "come inside our framework and discuss."The "U" culture says -"please can we agree to discuss detailed item number one on the agenda, then detailed item number two?
>
> That is why we never start talking.[4]

In addition, among the speakers describing inter-cultural differences in dealing with conflicts was John Paul Lederach. He presented his thesis on a Latin American model of mediating. He observed that rather than looking for an independent, neutral conflict specialist with an emphasis on tasks and a short term commitment, Latinos tend to look for someone who knows the parties, is fair, and is likely to be available for the long term and is focused on relationships, such as a priest.

The next step in the development of cultural awareness was to move from describing differences to doing something about them. The 1989 NCPCR conference in Montreal provided the next window on the field's progress. NCPCR had become an international forum. At this conference, an anthropology student from Bryn Mawr, Jennifer Spruill, presented work she had done during a summer internship with me. She had developed the first cross-cultural training module available for use by community mediation programs. While a few program trainers had developed some cross-cultural training capacity, they were not sharing the materials. We sold Spruill's packet for the mere sum of $4.00.

In addition, John Paul Lederach made a presentation introducing his concept of elicitative training for conflict resolution work in different countries and cultures. His groundbreaking model, built on his Latin American experience, involves running seminars in which the participants are asked what concepts and metaphors for conflict are expressed in their culture and community.

This model rested on a new view of mediation in which the cultural metaphors become important focal points for training conflict resolvers. For instance, starting from the understanding that Nicaraguan metaphors for conflict involve being entangled in conflict, and straightening out conflicts, he observed that Latin Americans think in terms of disentangling relationships. Standard North American training that is issue oriented was not appropriate. Rather, the trainer needs to probe the trainees for experiences of someone successfully untangling a conflict. What worked? What did not? This approach uncovers the culturally relevant models for the trainers to use.

Lederach's innovation still is used widely over a decade later. The elicitative approach to training is emphasized strongly by Eastern Mennonite University, where Lederach chaired the graduate program in conflict transformation before moving to Notre Dame.

Questions about Diversity

After the Montreal NCPCR in 1989, the essential ingredients for achieving diversity on the local program level were in place. The concept that cultural differences affect the way people handle their conflicts was accepted, as was the idea that location and program structure impact on who participates. Further, training and mediation models that were culturally sensitive had become available. The tools were there, and utilized. The field became more diverse, but not necessarily inclusive.

There was a strong element of "we" (white middle class organizers) reaching out to "them" (minorities, people of color, etc.). "We" wanted "them" to participate in "our" process. For the most part, the white program leaders held on to their directorates and leadership positions. This meant that minorities were empowered to participate, but not to shape programs to fit their own community's needs.

In the 1990s, we began to see people of color wresting ownership of conflict resolution processes from the pioneering white program staff. An illustrative case was a joint project of the Pittsburgh Mediation Center, Duquesne University, and the CISP Program (Community Intensive Supervision Program), an alternative program for youthful offenders. The partners developed a training program to be conducted in and with the African American community. The goals were to train mediators in order to institutionalize mediation in Pittsburgh's black community. Since they were hoping that some of the newly trained mediators would join the roster at Pittsburgh Mediation Center, the training was based on the center's standard curriculum interlaced with role plays keyed to the problems faced by youth workers in a gang infested environment.

At the outset of the training program, the trainers were delighted with the diversity among the first group of trainees. The trainers were optimistic that these trainees would use their skills beyond the young offender program. However some saw it differently. One trainee expressed the disempowerment she experienced in this situation.

> The trainers were just giving words to things we were already doing. You disrespect people who have been working in the field for 15 years when you tell them, "I'm going to give you something new. This is the way you do it." In reality we've been saving lives for 15 years. It looks like someone just came up with a bunch of catch phrases to get money to use to organize around....You presume community people don't know how to do this. It's like, "They didn't get their grass cut before you invented the lawn mower."[5]

Distrust grew, and soon the training ground to a halt. Trainees and trainers sat down together and "we went through all the stages of development: storming, norming and transforming. We had to take into account the different mindsets, cultural and racial differences. We examined where we met, how long we met and what went on at meetings".[6] Together the trainers and trainees built a new training program. Its structures and content reflected the needs and culture of the African American participants. The community trainees, having participated in redesigning the program , felt vested in it and empowered to spread conflict resolution skills through their community by training others.

Local programs, that had experiences like the Pittsburgh one, learned that diversity means more than just inviting others to work with us. That approach leaves the minorities disempowered, with a foot in the door but the rest of the body outside. The next step, which the Pittsburgh group began, is to develop an inclusive organization; one in which it is no longer "us" and "them". The program must be owned and be responsive to all involved. Differences are valued and no single culture predominates.

We can examine this transition by tracing the development of NCPCR through three consecutive conferences geared towards diversity: 1993, 1995, and 1997.

1. Daniel P. Joyce, *Conflict Resolution and Communities of Color: A Grass-Roots Culturally Defined Approach*, Manuscript presented at NCPCR, 1995

2. Paul Wahrhaftig, *It's Who you Know – Not What's Needed: Problems in Organizing Conflict Resolution Networks*, Manuscript, 1983, p. 1

3. Paul Wahrhaftig, "Alternatives to Mediation/Arbitration", *The Mooter*, Vol. 1, No. 3, 1978, p. 25 (excerpted)

4. Peter McLachlan, "Northern Ireland; The Cultural Bases of the Conflict," *Conflict Resolution Notes*, Vol. 4, No. 3, 1987, p. 21-22

5. Paul Wahrhaftig, "Norming, Storming and Forming a Gang Related Model for Conflict Resolution," *Conflict Resolution Notes*, Vol. 15, Nos. 1-2, September 1997, p. 9

6. *Ibid*. p. 9-10

CHAPTER 8 — SALT AND PEPPER ISN'T ENOUGH-INSTITUTIONAL CHANGE: DIVERSITY TO INCLUSIVENESS, NCPCR EXPERIENCE

We have reviewed the stages from gradual awakening, to understanding cultural differences, to integration, and to diversity issues, as CDR programs sought to empower disenfranchised communities. However, salt and pepper integration is only one step on the way to building truly empowering institutions. This awakening can be illustrated by reviewing the diversity-to-inclusiveness developments of the National Conference on Peacemaking and Conflict Resolution (NCPCR), now known as *PeaceWeb*.

Why choose NCPCR for this focus? First, NCPCR was a major national presence. Its conferences reached out to and welcomed community mediators. For over two decades NCPCR supported, challenged, and gave voice to the CDR programs through its bi-annual national conferences. It welcomed and promoted the view that conflict resolution is more than a profession; it is social movement. The empowerment process cannot be just the concern of local organizations. Racism and other excluding-isms, are a national problem and need to be confronted on that scale.

Second, most of NCPCR's struggles over the sensitive issues of racial exclusion were in the open and in public view. It would be much more difficult to reconstruct as much information about the struggles of a local program.[1] NCPCR's progress in building an inclusive organization parallels and foreshadows the diversity activities of many local CDR programs. The concerns are the same. Organizations seeking to help empower communities (or empower local organizations that seek to empower communities) should benefit from the involvement and insight of members of those communities.

Third, I was a part of NCPCR's leadership for much of the period covered in this account. Having served on conference committees for NCPCR2 (St. Louis, '84) and NCPCR 3(Denver '86) and as coordinator of international participants for NCPCR4 in Montreal ('89), I was elected to NCPCR's board in 1989. In 1991, I was elected chair of the board for two consecutive two-year terms. Stepping down from the chair in 1995, I became co-chair of the local conference committee for the 1997 Pittsburgh NCPCR, after which I was rotated off the board. Thus, I can write with an insider's insight, but also with some insider shortcomings. Further, my perspective is that of a European American. No matter how inclusive, fair and insightful I try to be, inevitably I view these developments through dominant culture filters.

Looking back on my experiences and observations, I would suggest that successful struggles to build inclusive, empowering organizations include a series of steps.

1. The institution has to become aware that there is a problem.
2. It recruits and involves targeted groups to participate in the existing program, leading to integration.
3. As participation reaches critical mass, challenges to the dominant culture arise.
4. Recognizing the need for institutional cultural and leadership change, the program embarks on appropriate paths.
5. As change begins to be incorporated into the institutional culture, the program becomes fragile and crisis prone.
6. A new, stable culture emerges.

Beyond Integration

NCPCR conferences provided an opportunity to take a bi-annual inventory of the field, to chronicle developments, and to challenge participants to explore new ideas. I have already reviewed the gradual awakening of the CDR field to the fact that different cultures handle conflicts differently. That awakening led to awareness of the need to involve people from the communities that the programs were seeking to empower. CDR programs began to become integrated but were not yet inclusive. Integration, as I am using it, sends a message, "Come participate in *my* institution". An inclusive organization's message is "Let's work together in *our* institution". Who owns the program is the difference in the two formulations.

Awareness

Until the 1989 conference in Montreal, participants struggled to understand the impact of culture on the disputing process and even on the need for CDR programs to improve the racial diversity of their boards of directors and mediator pools. Few of NCPCR's European American participants saw that racism was built into the fabric of the conferences. While over the years NCPCR had attracted a higher percentage of participants of color than any of the conferences put on by the other national organizations,* the board apparently felt no need to make any significant changes to promote broader participation in the organization and its governance. That began to change in 1989.

There were enough people of color attending the 1989 Montreal conference to come together in caucuses and begin to raise issues about why there were so few minorities present. They pointed out that holding the conference in Montreal, especially in mid-winter, raised significant barriers to potential participants who lacked travel funds. The location was remote from major African American or Hispanic population centers.

NCPCR's response was two-fold. First, they chose a new board of directors. That is when I became a director, along with Timothy Germany, the only person of color on the 15-person board. The board also chose Charlotte, North Carolina for the next conference reasoning that by locating the conference in the South, with its high concentration of African Americans, more people of color would be able to attend. Further, North Carolina had a promising state association of mediation programs that would help recruit diverse attendees.

The 1991 NCPCR at Charlotte became a disappointment from the diversity perspective. There was a change of leadership in The

---

* Society of Professionals in Dispute Resolution (SPIDR), Academy of Family Mediators (AFM), National Association for Mediation in Education (NAME), Association of Family and Conciliation Courts (AFCC).

Mediation Network of North Carolina that had agreed to host the conference and play an active role in recruiting local participants They virtually dropped out of the conference. The result was that attendance from the immediate area, the target area with a high African American population, was low. The conference hotel was too expensive for many, and the only inexpensive alternative housing was far across the city, with poor public transportation. To add insult to injury, the conference hotel was located in a magnificent, newly built urban redevelopment area that had been the heart of Charlotte's African American community. We were staying in a living monument to the proposition that "Urban Renewal Means Negro Removal".

At this conference the people of color met again in caucuses, and their complaints filtered up to the board, mainly through informal sidebar conversations. A new board was installed, based on a slate brought in by the board's nominating committee. The process followed standard NCPCR procedure. About six months before the conference, a nominating committee developed a slate that was voted on by the board before the conference; the results were announced at the end of the conference. The result: Timothy Germany remained the sole person of color on the board, and I was elected to chair the board. When we met for the first time, at the end of the conference, there was enough dissatisfaction about the level of diversity in the conference and the board, that we decided to devote the next conference (1993) to exploring diversity issues.

The exploration of diversity issues was much more complex than just responding to the concerns of people of color. Other groups felt excluded or diminished by NCPCR and the CR field in general. In deciding to focus on "diversity" rather than "racism", NCPCR created a vehicle for confronting issues of gender preference, and disabilities, as well as racism. However, my focus in this account is on racism: the deepest, and most pervasive and complex of the "isms". It should be noted however, that the other "isms" traveled on a parallel track, but with slightly different timing. For instance, gays and lesbians were caucusing and beginning to communicate their frustrations at about the same time that people of color were finding their voice. The board, elected in 1991, included one gay and one lesbian member.

Leading up to the 1993 Portland conference, I appointed a nominating committee with the usual task of developing a slate of new members to be voted on before the conference. Further, I charged them, and requested the rest of the board to help them, to bring back a slate that would increase the board membership of people of color.

To my dismay, when the nominating committee presented its slate, the candidates were all white folks. Neither the nominating committee nor any board members, myself included, had identified a person of color with appropriate qualifications for a leadership position. It was too late to send the slate back to the nominating committee, because it would have been impossible to squeeze in the election in the few days before the conference. I polled the board as to what to do. The idea of going into a conference with a diversity theme with only a token person of color on the board, was unacceptable. But time had run out on the election procedure.

Julianna Birkhoff, a board member and, at that time, a doctoral candidate in George Mason University's Institute for Conflict Analysis and Resolution, insisted that if we were serious about combating racism, then we must step out of the business-as-usual mode. If the new slate was not ready in time for the usual election, change something. We did.

I gave the opening speech at the conference. The audience was the most racially diverse to attend any NCPCR up to that time. I spoke of the nominating problem we were experiencing and announced that we would reject the all white slate. I appealed to the conference to become the nominating committee of the whole and requested that anyone submit names of persons of color for board membership consideration. The board would hold the nominations open for a few weeks after the conference and then would elect a new board.

Before the end of the conference, I had received a list of about twenty people of color who would be available. We held an emergency board meeting near the end of the conference to review the submissions. That was when the real anguish began for me. I had to acknowledge that an organization that I led had been unable to break through the racial barriers. I wrote all the names from the list on a flip chart. We considered each name one at a time. I asked, "Who knows this person? Tell us about him or her". Despite the fact that a few weeks earlier this board had been totally unable to think of a single person of color who could contribute to the board, each name on the list was familiar to at least one board member. Further, many of the names submitted would (and did) make excellent board members.

Need for Institutional Change

At the closing ceremonies of the conference, I tearfully reported on the status of the nomination process. It was difficult to admit before a packed auditorium that not only was institutional racism involved, but there was a need for personal work focused on individual racism. This need was clear and indicated by the fact that so many of our colleagues of color had been "invisible" to us. It was both a low point in my career and a high point. Low, because I had to acknowledge my blindness to my colleagues of color. High, because we had broken through a major barrier and finally were able to move forward, both institutionally and personally, towards inclusion. I had no idea how long and rocky that road would be.

Within a few weeks, we had a new board in place with much wider diversity, thanks to the list developed at the conference. The new board consisted of fifteen people, including seven women, three gay or lesbian, three people of color.

Looking to build on the Portland experience, the new board agreed that the next conference also would focus on diversity, highlighting institutional dimensions. We attracted a creative pair to co-chair the conference committee, Beth Roy and Mary Adams Trujillo. They represented racial and sexual preference diversity, and, more importantly, great creativity. Their creativity was overwhelming to me since I felt responsibility, as chair of the board, for assuring that the organization used its resources well and survived.

The first issue that the new conference chairs brought to the board was a request to expand the conference committee beyond its current fifteen members and to meet with them more frequently than past conference committees. Though meetings of a national committee of that size were very expensive, Roy and Trujillo convinced us that we needed a larger committee to have enough minority representation, and additional meeting time would be required for participants to feel empowered to make their perspectives known. Further, the committee would serve as an entry route to bringing more minorities into the conference and the organization. We hoped that committee members would later become board members. They did.

The composition of the new, expanded conference committee of 20 people was: 12 women, including seven people of color (African American, Native American, Hispanic and Korean), 2 gay and 2 physically challenged.

From its inception, the National Conference Committee set out to change NCPCR's institutional culture. Beth Roy, co-chair of the committee, observed that NCPCR was taking institutional change seriously. It had effectively ceded power and control to this committee of people who were new to the organization.[2] I had accepted a second term as board chair, to help navigate NCPCR through this period of change. I also attended the national conference committee meetings *ex officio*. As I was balancing between keeping NCPCR solvent and allowing flexibility for major change, I felt like I had one foot on the shore and the other in a whirlpool of change.

Time and Culture

The first meeting of this committee was in Tempe, Arizona. It began at 9:30 in the morning. I remember taking a break at around 2 PM and realizing we were still on agenda item #1: "Introduce yourself and tell us a little about what brings you here". When were we going to get something done? Of course, what we were doing was building the relationships necessary for functioning in such a diverse group. This was one of the first important steps in organizational culture change for NCPCR. We recognized that tight deadlines clash with relationship building issues, which are at the heart of diversity work.

Cultures do not change overnight. This committee experience was only the beginning of an extended period of experimentation with the proper balance between relationship building and deadline adherence. It took years to work out that balance. By the second conference committee meeting, I began to discover that in spite of, or perhaps because of, the emphasis on relationship building, deadlines were met.

Some advantages of the new diversity appeared almost immediately. The second committee meeting was a day and a half of intense work sitting around a large table. Rather than have one person leading or facilitating the whole meeting, at each break a different person would step forward to facilitate. Most of the committee members were experienced facilitators, but with a wide variety of styles. The person selected to lead after each break somehow had a style that fit the needs of the moment. Early in the day facilitators tended to be very relationship oriented. Towards the end of the day, when a lot of decisions had to be made, the facilitator for a session would be a more directive, goal oriented person. When tensions mounted, in came a facilitator to take the lead and use soothing background music to calm our nerves.

NCPCR was in the beginning stages of a major internal cultural transition. It was re-interpreting basic concepts of time, task orientation, and group process. It was embarking on internal change at the same time that it was shifting its external relations; that is, how NCPCR would relate to the rapidly changing world of conflict resolvers. It was increasingly clear that NCPCR's standard programming format was becoming obsolete. Its main function was to hold a bi-annual conference that brought together diverse elements of the field of conflict resolution and, in particular, supported community dispute resolution programs. Other national, state and regional organizations were now holding conferences of good quality that were less expensive to attend. NCPCR needed to change its conference format drastically to fit the new needs of the field. It had to determine what it would take to make the large conference more competitive, attracting enough participants to maintain adequate revenue. Or, it needed to find other activities to supplement its work. For example, it could market its conference planning expertise to some of the emerging conferences.

Some changes were evident at the 1995 Minneapolis conference. It was the most diverse group of participants by far. People of color, people with disabilities, and people of various sexual preferences played leading roles in all aspects of the conference. New innovations appeared, such as a quiet room to which participants could retreat for contemplation and relief from the highly stimulating conference.

But there continued to be some complaints, echoing those at Portland two years earlier. The conference hotel was too expensive and opulent, and Minneapolis had a very low population of people of color. These two problems had persisted because of outside constraints. Conference locations must be chosen three or more years ahead in order to reserve good conference space. Portland and Minneapolis had been chosen years ahead based on criteria unrelated to the move towards diversity. The location of the next conference would reflect the thinking of the newly diverse board.

The choice of Pittsburgh, Pennsylvania for the next conference, scheduled for 1997 was rooted in diversity concerns. The conference was to be held at Duquesne University, which was accessible from both downtown and major African American communities. Pittsburgh had a significant black population. Further, inexpensive dormitory rooms were the standard housing for the conference attendees, with only a few opting for nearby hotels.

MACK Truck and a Bumpy Transition

The planning for the 1997 Pittsburgh conference was first enriched and later paralyzed, by the fluid stage of NCPCR's culture. To attract as broad a spectrum as possible in both the planning and implementation, NCPCR expanded the relevant committees and leadership. There was a conference committee constituted on a national scale, and a local committee that traditionally organized hospitality. All committees were responsible to the board of directors. The Pittsburgh planning involved these same three groups but with expanded and highly diverse membership. Rather than a single convener or chair, the local committee, the national conference committee and the board each had co-chairs. In fact, the National Conference Committee had three chairs. Further complicating the situation, it was unclear what the jurisdiction of each committee was and where decision making responsibility lay.

To compound this complex arrangement, inter-racial trust was really just beginning to evolve after years of lip service to matters of diversity and inclusion. Most of us had underestimated how difficult it is to function inclusively. We could meet and do the business of a committee reasonably well. However, when we would tire late in the day, or relax a little, incredible misunderstandings would bubble to the surface, needing resolution. Board meetings now functioned with more time devoted to relationship building and less to moving through agendas and meeting time constraints. The conference was a wreck waiting to happen.

I was no longer on the board, having reached my term limit. However, I attended as co-chair of the Pittsburgh local committee. I remember one meeting in particular where the relationship focus was requiring so much time that we did not address key decisions that I felt we needed to make to meet important deadlines for the Pittsburgh conference. It looked like the issues would not even come to the floor. A lengthy discussion was winding along about setting the date for the next meeting. Then the board embarked on an endless discussion about how it felt to make that decision. I blurted out a few explicatives, and added that I felt like I was walking up a narrow alley while ahead of me an 18-wheel Mack Truck was coming right at me. I could see that the people in the cab were totally engaged in discussing what color the horn-ring should be. I was in near panic that the conference would crash.

The truck hit, but later. The death of a black man at the hands of suburban police in the Pittsburgh area, combined with the release of a study documenting extremely high racially based economic inequalities in Pittsburgh, created ferment in Pittsburgh's black community. A new group surfaced, Concerned Black Citizens (CBC), from the community calling for a boycott of downtown businesses and cancel all conventions scheduled for Pittsburgh until their grievances were met. About six weeks before the conference, they asked NCPCR to cancel or move the conference to another city.

Moving the conference at the last minute, if it were possible, would have incured high costs. Among them would be liability for breach of contract with the university conference site and conference related hotels, heavy logistical costs of notifying the thousands on the mailing list of the change, and significant disruption of travel plans that could involve airline ticket surcharges. Damage to the reputations of the local organizations that had invested heavily in developing the conference would have been significant. It probably would have closed down my program. The Conflict Resolution Center International, of which I was President, had invested over two years of its programming on conference related activities. We had raised funds, brought together organized labor and management to conduct a panel, and arranged to train news staff from the major news outlets in how to report on conflicts constructively. Most of the people involved in these activities would never understand why this conference, which we had vouched, for, had pulled out.

Costs of ignoring the boycott would have been significant, also. It would damage the credibility of Concerned Black Citizens, and discourage attendance by those unwilling to cross a picket line, thus reducing revenue. It would put the conference in the awkward position of promoting diversity and inclusiveness while being picketed by a black organization.

Meanwhile, rumors were spreading among NCPCR's constituency, leaving potential participants in a quandary as to whether to make airline reservations. An information sheet was developed to be mailed to all perspective attendees giving them solid information on which to base their decisions. However, that mailing was delayed until decisions had been made about whether to hold the conference, and how to word the mailing.

The boycott raised multiple issues, all of which involved unresolved internal diversity problems within NCPCR. Some of these were:

1. Where does decision making lie in the organization? Who or which committees can make a decision on the boycott issue?
2. Should NCPCR negotiate with Concerned Black Citizens? If so, who is trusted enough to do it? Should it be an all black negotiating team or mixed? Pittsburghers or outsiders?
3. Can an organization, which values consensus decision making reach agreement quickly enough to deal with a fluid situation like this? Once the right committee is empowered to make a decision, NCPCR traditionally made decisions using a consensus process. All members of the appropriate body had to agree before a decision was final. While consensus decision making may produce better quality agreements, it tends to be a slow process
4. Who decides which of the many voices authentically speaks for Pittsburgh's black community? There was a major split on the boycott issue among local black organizations involved in the conference planning. Some wanted the infusion of skills that would come with the conference, and others aligned with Concerned Black Citizens. Should Pittsburghers be trusted to make the decision or should out-of- town board members make a fact-finding trip to Pittsburgh?
5. Should an organization of conflict resolvers offer to serve as a potential mediator among the factions of Pittsburgh's black community, or should it ally with a faction, based on social justice positions, and if so, which faction?

After an extensive and bitter debate, by email and conference calls, the board agreed to a negotiating position and developed an agreement with CBC. The terms of the agreement were:

1. The conference would remain in place.
2. CBC was invited to address the conference to publicize its perspective.
3. NCPCR would hold a closed seminar on constructive and safe policing with black community representatives, politicians and the police.
4. NCPCR would inform attendees of the downtown boycott and would distribute information about black owned restaurants and places to eat outside the boycotted areas of the city.
5. CBC agreed that Duquesne University, the conference site, was not within the zone defined as "downtown" and thus was not subject to the boycott.

The conference went forward amid discussions of whether the agreement was appropriate, a sell out, or too activist. Ultimately, the controversy gave context to the conference's emphasis on building integrative institutions.

Emerging Culture

At the conclusion of the Pittsburgh conference most of the "old" board members were due to rotate off. The new board was even more diverse than the last. Their interest in diversity and inclusiveness issues resulted in NCPCR shifting its organizational focus to concentrate mainly on those issues. Subsequent conferences were strong on diversity and increasingly weak on other community conflict resolution issues. NCPCR changed its name to Network of Communities for Peacemaking and Conflict Resolution (still NCPCR), and now is known also as "Peaceweb."

These new directions were consistent with the conclusion the board had come to over the years; that it was time for a change. Whether or not the organization had undergone this diversification process, change would have been called for. It is natural that revisions reflected the interests of the newly empowered board members.

Roberto Chene, a member of the board and a diversity consultant, reflected on the NCPCR experience. He summed it up by saying that NCPCR had recruited him and others to enter a change process, and the agency had nourished the newcomers throughout. Going into this process, he felt the group believed it could diversify without conflict and that this group was particularly well qualified to make the transition to a true multicultural organization. After going through the process and the controversies, he feels that we still do not know much about how best to move an organization in the right direction. Each situation is unique.[3]

Just as there is no single road to racial inclusiveness, there are many paths to reach community empowerment. The important lesson is that both must be done consciously and carefully. Failure to attend to these issues will result in a default situation, racial exclusiveness, and ownership and control of CDR programs becoming appendages of the courts.

1. For an insightful look at one CDR program's approach to achieving inclusiveness, see, Melinda Smith, "Diversity in Community Mediation: A Conversation with Janice Tudy-Jackson and Roberto Chene," *Mediation Quarterly*, Vol. 17 No. 4, 2000, p. 369
2. Beth Roy, Comments at Praxis Seminar, NCPCR, April 2, 2003
3. Roberto Chene, Comments at Praxis Seminar, NCPCR, April 2, 2003

CHAPTER 9 — THE GLOBAL CONFLICT RESOLUTION MOVEMENT

International Role

The evolution of my thinking from criminal justice reform to community empowerment to peace building has been reflected in my international work. The tumultuous events of the collapse of the Soviet Union, and its ripple effect on the rest of the world, created an opening and a demand for conflict resolution work. Many American CDR organizers found useful applications and fertile markets for their skills in troubled, newly independent countries.

For example, Ray Shonholtz resigned his position as Executive Director of Community Boards Program in San Francisco and founded Partners for Democratic Change (PDC). PDC established centers in former Iron Curtain countries to study, train, and implement mediation and conflict resolution programs at whatever level of society was most in need or was most ripe for these skills. Centers were created in Poland, Bulgaria, Albania, Czech Republic, Georgia, Hungary, Kosovo, Lithuania, Romania, and Slovakia, all trained in the Community Board conciliation model. Centers then were free to adapt the model to their cultural and political needs, but, since they had a common training experience, it was hoped that they would retain a common conflict resolution language.

I was involved in transnational networking of conflict resolution information almost from the beginning of my work. As that emphasis began to expand, I reconstituted my program in 1981, as the Conflict Resolution Center International, an independent, not-for-profit organization. In the early period, I responded to inquiries about CDR by providing information about how it was done in the USA, since that was all the information I had. Two early examples were Australia and South Africa. Stella Cornelius, then a volunteer with the United Nations Association in Australia, and H. W. van de Merwe, of the University of Cape Town, both collected as much information about the American CDR models as they could find and then they modified these to fit their countries' culture and current political needs.

I was also an information source for the British CDR movement that is now coordinated by a national resource center, Mediation UK. Similarly, my experience bringing Janaki Mahendran and Jonathan Gosling from London's *Newham Conflict and Change Program*, to the 1984 St. Louis NCPCR conference was an excellent reminder that networking involves a two-way flow of ideas. While the Newham representatives studied and learned new approaches from the Americans, they also inspired the Americans with their unique approach to conflict resolution work.

I was pushing the American empowerment model, particularly the community organizing approach, until I began to see that this orientation simply did not work in many other societies. The empowerment model made sense in the USA because of our particular culture and history. The tumult of the peace and civil rights movement were essential in instilling a distrust of government institutions and a sense that civil society organizing can promote change.

Canadians, for instance, while adapting the American model for the most part, tend to be more trusting of the government and courts. The resulting programs are much more closely related to the courts than their American community counterparts. They render a good service, empowering the parties to manage their own conflicts, but they put less emphasis on empowerment beyond the confines of the dispute.

Most of the people I worked with in France could not relate to the concept of an independent community initiated and run project. France has a strong tradition of a centralized governmental bureaucracy. Specifically, social programming starts at the ministerial level and filters down to the local. They evolved their own organizing methodology.

I gradually changed my approach to listening and learning more and encouraging people I worked with to find the essential principles underlying the work we do in America. They could see then whether and how those principles might be applied in their country.

Technology Transfers

For example, at the 1989 NCPCR in Montreal, I was serving as host for overseas participants. Near the close of the conference, I convened the visitors and asked for an assessment of the conference. Most lauded the depth and variety of information available about all facets of conflict resolution in North America. However, a Nigerian chief, in flowing robes, stated with great dignity, "Yes, there is plenty of information here that we can take home with us and use. But I feel technology transfers from the "developed" world have victimized my country time and time again. And this is a technology transfer".

I replied, "I recognize your concern, but I think there is something in the history of the American models that you may not know. The origin of our CDR work grows out of the reports of anthropologists who documented the informal conflict settlement processes in Latin America and Africa. So what you see at this conference is the result of a technology transfer from the Third World to North America. We looked at the African and Latin American experiences with village elders rendering informal justice. We filtered our observations through our cultural lenses and created a model that fit our society. For example, in most African village conflict resolution processes the intervenor is someone with prestige and power. The nearest concept we could find to describe that role was "mediator". As soon as we used that label, then a whole cluster of cultural values applied, such as the "mediator" must be neutral and hold no power over the parties.

"So," I continued, "if you want to look at the American model, note how it has been adapted as part of the technology transfer from your society to ours. And then see if there are any fundamental principles that you might want to transfer back home".

The chief must have found some value from this technology transfer. He maintained a subscription to my periodical for his peace center until I ceased publication in 2004.

A mediator's stock answer to most questions is "It all depends…." The answer in technology transfer as well as empowerment is "It all depends…." If we look at the details, the implementation plans, *it all depends*. But if we look at widely accepted underlying principles, such as, *people can play a major role in solving their own problems*, or *democratic processes are desirable for a healthy society*, we will find common understandings. Propositions like these are the core of mediation. The fancy techniques to implement these core understandings are likely to vary significantly in different cultures.

I had the opportunity to participate in and observe the potential that mediation activities have on empowering people to participate in newly formed democracies. I developed an increasing respect for the potential impact of the conflict resolution movement around the globe. The potential is exciting, as long as we do not lose track of empowerment issues.

For example, during the Balkan wars of the 1990s, I developed a relationship with Project MOST of the Centre for Anti-War Action, Belgrade. Njeza Mrse, my main contact, was busy doing conflict resolution work. She was not directly mediating the war situation since she did not have high level access. Rather she worked in refugee camps, helping people cope with the trauma from their war experiences. Her reasoning was that she could have an impact on this level. And further, if the spiral of Balkan Wars is not broken, then repeat wars are inevitable. Working with refugees, assisting, and training them in conflict resolution has the potential of reducing animosity and breaking the cycle. She blended psychological and conflict resolution approaches to help refugee women resettle. Others in Project MOST studied conflict resolution and applied it where they could, often in school settings.

CR as a Democratic Skill

I visited Belgrade, Yugoslavia, in 2001, one year after the fall of the Milosevic government and its replacement by a reformist coalition. It was clear that the new government recognized the importance of the collaborative democratic skills that these mediators and therapists had been transmitting. Njeza Mrse was finishing writing a job description for her new post in the Ministry of Education. She would be running a series of workshops, based on her CR skills, teaching the pragmatic work of democracy, such as how to run a non-authoritarian meeting. Her co-worker, Gordana Miljevic, had been appointed the Director of External Relations for the Ministry of Education.

It was most apparent that the new regime saw conflict resolution training as a valuable resource for empowering citizens to take part in a democracy. A few individuals can make a difference.

We can help empower individuals in a mediation setting. We can aim at empowering neighborhoods, cities, and even countries. Why not the world? That is the next challenge. The global community of the 21st Century will involve linking communities around the world. A new project, the Global Partnership to Prevent Armed Conflict, is taking the lead in linking local activities with global resources. Its overall objective is to develop a common platform for effective action in conflict prevention, from the community to the global level. To accomplish its goals, the Partnership is calling for regional workshops to discuss the role of civil society in conflict resolution and to strengthen ties among conflict resolvers. The findings of the regional conferences will be fed into a major international conference sponsored by the United Nations.

Another sense of empowerment may apply here. We in the CR field have begun to feel empowered sufficiently to widen our horizons and explore the global peace-building potential of our communities and conflict resolution programs. Or as the Global Partnership News, March 2004 stated:

> In the last two decades, civil society has become an active player in the areas of human rights, environment, development, co-operation and related areas. The international campaign to ban landmines and the campaign for the International Criminal Court have shown that civil society organizations can carry major international efforts - but not on their own. Key to the success and impact of the campaign against landmines and the effort to establish the ICC has been effective coalition building among various disparate NGOs, governments, international organizations and the UN. It is now time that these examples are emulated in the area of conflict prevention.[1]

Conclusion

After exploring the wide range of empowerment, social change, and peace-building potential of CDR programs, whether viewed locally or globally, it is a loss to our society when program directors see only the direct service implications of their work. When people develop, change or modify any social program, there will be an impact on society beyond its immediate scope. Sometimes this is called *unintended consequences*. It would be preferable to assess what sort of change a CDR program would like to affect, and then structure the services to be consistent with the program's "intended consequences".

This book is my attempt to answer the questions, "What is empowerment, and how can it be done"? This exploration suggests that *it all depends* on such considerations as:

- Whom are we trying to empower?
- For what purpose?
- What is the overall social climate?
- What resources are there to work with?

CDR, as an alternative to the criminal justice system, can empower the parties to make decisions about their own dispute. Programs that see the community building potential can use the information and experiences accumulated from mediation sessions to organize community responses to identified problems. The Northern Irish have demonstrated that CDR can be an effective tool for creating a culture of peace, even in a war torn society.

These answers are much more complicated than ones I would have given when I started writing this work. I would have emphasized the community-organizing model typified by Community Boards, Cleveland Mediation Center, and Community Association for Mediation. Similarly, I would have castigated program directors that deviated from that model as having lost the vision of the founders. However, as I reflected on the range of experiences highlighted here, I see clearly that, "It all depends ..." Just as a mediator does not prescribe solutions but focuses the parties onto key issues they must work with, I can only urge people involved in CDR to recognize that their program can be a resource for social change if they will pursue techniques and approaches that implement that agenda.

Postlogue

In the words of the Canadian pioneer in the community mediation field, Dean Peachey:

> Thinking about what we are trying to accomplish in changing attitudes, relationships and power, collectively we have not done a good job advancing our vision. It is part of a broader vision of understanding our lives, our purpose, our meaning on this earth. As an old saying goes, 'There is no time for anything in this life, except to make peacework part of every moment.' In our own way we each take a step in the direction of peace. We see elements of success; we see elements that are disheartening, such as more violence on television and military activities. We do what we can to articulate and live toward our vision. It is exciting, it is exhausting, and it can be energizing.[2]

1. Editor, "International Developments," *Global Partnership for the Prevention of Armed Conflict News*, March 2004, p. 1

2. Dean Peachey, Remarks made in workshop, *Strengthening Communities Through Community Dispute Resolution Programs at the conference Interaction 2004, Conflict Resolution Network*, Canada, June 4, 2004

INDEX

BIBLIOGRAPHY

AMERICAN FRIENDS SERVICE COMMITTEE, *Struggle For Justice: A Report On Crime And Punishment In America*. Hill and Wang, 1971

BEER, JENNIFER and E. EILEEN STIEF, *The Mediator's Handbook, 3ʳᵈ Edition*, New Society Press, 1994

BRODER, JOAN, "Mediation in Ireland", *Conflict Resolution Notes*, Vol. 6, No. 4, 1989, p 79

BELL GRIFFIN B., Address to Mexican-American Legal Defense Fund, February 15, 1977

_____, Press Release, July 28, 1977

BOBROWSKY, KIM, E-mail message to Paul Wahrhaftig, June 3, 2004

BRADLEY, SCOTT and MELINDA SMITH, "Community Mediation: Reflections on a Quarter Century of Practice", *Mediation Quarterly*, Vol. 17, No. 4, Summer 2000, p. 315

BURGER, WARREN E., "Our Viscious Legal Spiral", *The Judges Journal*, Vol. 16, No. 4, Fall 1977, p 48

BUSH, ROBERT A. BARUCH and JOSEPH P. FOLGER, *The Promise of Mediation, Responding to Conflict Through Empowerment and Recognition*, Jossey-Bass, 1994

CHENE, ROBERTO, Comments at Praxis Seminar, NCPCR, April 2, 2003

CHRISTIE, NILES, "Conflicts as Property", *The British Journal of Criminology*, Vol. 17, No. 1, January 1977, p.1

DAVIS, ALBIE, "How to Ensure High Quality Mediation Services: the Issue of Credentialing," in *Community Mediation Handbook*, Karen Duffey, James W. Grovner, and Paul V Olczak, (eds.), Guilford Press, NY, 1991, p. 203

DUBOW, FRED, "Evaluating Community Based Conflict Resolution Programs", *Conflict Resolution Notes*, Vol. 2, No. 3, 1985, p. 25

DUNN, EDGAR, "Arbitration as an Alternative to District Courts", *The Citizen Dispute Organizer's Handbook*, Paul Wahrhaftig, ed., 1981, p. 30

EDITOR, "International Developments", *Global Partnership for the Prevention of Armed Conflict News*, March 2004, p. 1

EDITOR,"Spreading the 'Peace Virus'", *Ottawa Citizen*, page D4, April 10, 1998, as posted at http://www.webnet/nccr/citizen.html

FOLGER, JOSEPH, "Empowerment: Self Determination or Altruistic Persuasion?" *Conflict Resolution Notes*, Vol. 8, No. 1, 1990, p. 1

JOYCE, DANIEL P., *Conflict Resolution and Communities of Color: A Grass-Roots Culturally Defined Approach*, Manuscript presented at NCPCR, 1995

_____, interview, December 13, 2002

KING, MARTIN LUTHER JR, "Beyond Vietnam", April 4, 1967, http://www/ratical.com/ratville/JFK/MLKapr67.html

LAZERSON, MARK H, "In the Halls of Justice, the Only Justice Is in the Halls", *The Politics of Informal Justice*, Vol 1, Richard Able, ed., 1982, p. 119-160 at page 120

LOWY, MICHAEL J., *Basic Assumptions of Bail Reform and Pretrial Diversion – Some Alternatives*, Mimeograph by American Friends Service Committee, Pretrial Justice Federation, 1972

MERRY, SALLY and SUSAN SIBLEY, "What Do Plaintiffs Want?" *Justice Journal*, Vol. 9, No. 2, 1984

MCLACHLAN, PETER, "Northern Ireland; The Cultural Bases of the Conflict", *Conflict Resolution Notes*, Vol. 4, No. 3, 1987, p. 21

NEW YORK STATE UNIFIED COURT SYSTEM, OFFICE OF ALTERNATIVE DISPUTE RESOLUTION PROGRAMS, *Community Dispute Resolution Centers Program 2000-2002 Annual Report*

_____ *Community Dispute Resolution Centers Program, First Annual Report*, 1979

PEACHEY, DEAN, Remarks made in the workshop: *Strengthening Communities Through Community Dispute Resolution Programs* at the conference Interaction 2004, June 4, 2004

ROEHL, JANICE A., DAVID I. SHEPPARD, and ROYER F. COOK, *Neighborhood Justice Centers, Field Test: Final Evaluation Report – Executive Summary*, US Dept. of Justice, National Institute of Justice, 1980

ROY, BETH, Comments at Praxis Seminar, NCPCR, April 2, 2003

SACHS, ANDREW M., "Understanding Public Dispute Resolution in Community Mediation," *Mediation Quarterly*, Vol. 17, No. 4, Summer 2000, p. 341

SHONHOLTZ, RAYMOND, *The Citizens' Role in Justice: Building a Primary Justice and Prevention System at the Neighborhood Level*, Manuscript, 1987

SIEMENS, MARK, "Community Forum for Civil Discourse", *Conflict Resolution Notes*, Vol. 14, No. 4, 1996, p. 1

SMITH, MELINDA, "Diversity in Community Mediation: A Conversation with Janice Tudy-Jackson and Roberto Chene", *Mediation Quarterly*, Vol. 17, No. 4, 2000, p. 369

THOMAS, AVIS R., "Dialogue: Local to National", *Conflict Resolution Notes*, Vol. 15, No. 3, 1988, p. 20

WAHRHAFTIG, PAUL, "Alternatives to Mediation/Arbitration", *The Mooter,* Vol. 1, No. 3, 1978, p. 25

_____, "An Overview of Community-Oriented Citizen Dispute Resolution Programs in the United States", *The Politics of Informal Justice,* Vol. 1, p.75, Academic Press, 1982

_____, "Community Dispute Center New York – Some Observations", *The Citizen Dispute Organizer's Handbook*, Paul Wahrhaftig, ed., American Friends Service Committee, 1981, p. 33

_____, "Disputes Resolved in the Community", *Pretrial Justice Quarterly*, Vol. 2, No. 2, 1973, p. 1

_____, "Empowerment of Communities: A Philosophy Behind CDR Organizing,", *Mooter* Vol. 1, No. 1, 1977, p. 15

_____, *It's Who You Know – Not What's Needed: Problems in Organizing Conflict Resolution Networks*, Manuscript, 1983, p. 1

_____, Letter to Michael Lowy, October 19, 1976

_____, Letter to Nassau Coalition for Safety and Justice

_____, "Mediation at the Police Station", *Pretrial Justice Quarterly,* Vol. 3, No. 4, Fall 1974, p. 1

_____, "Norming, Storming and Forming a Gang Related Model for Conflict Resolution", *Conflict Resolution Notes,* Vol. 15, Nos. 1-2, September 1997, p. 9

RESOURCES AVAILABLE FROM NAFCM

PUBLICATIONS

Community Mediation Center Self-Assessment Manual
Based on over two years work of our quality assurance committee, this manual presents a range of questions, items for discussion, and resources intended to help centers determine for themselves what quality services really mean in their communities and contexts. Copyright © 2002.

Community Oriented Policing Curriculum (forthcoming)
Developed by NAFCM and the Bay Area Collaborative of mediation centers in Berkeley, Oakland, and San Francisco, CA, this curriculum shows how community mediation centers and community police can develop effective partnerships. Included are training materials for teaching conflict resolution and facilitation skills to police officers, and materials on police-youth partnerships.

Face to Face: Resolving Conflict Without Giving In or Giving Up
Face to Face is a modular curriculum developed by NAFCM to train AmeriCorps members. Modules address conflict at the personal level, conflict at the interpersonal level and provide concepts and tools for effective and collaborative intergroup and intragroup work. Copyright © 1996, 266 pp. plus workbook (81 pp.).

NAFCM Community Mediation Center Start-up Packet
A compilation of documents from the NAFCM Clearinghouse. The packet has the following sections: Principles for ADR Provider Organizations; A Guide to Getting Started; Office Basics; Personnel Guidelines, Policy, Ethics and Performance Review; Board of Directors/Governing Board; Volunteer Job Description, Mediation Form Examples; Skill-building Material for Mediators: Training Manual; Recipes for Successful Publications; Uniform Mediation Act.

Practice Notes

A collection of articles on mediation practice and mediation center management, collected from NAFCM's quarterly newsletter *The Community Mediator*. Written by long-time practitioner Ben Carroll, these 2-4 page articles provide condensed tips, insights, and directions to further reading on topics ranging from learning styles to preventing volunteer burn-out.

VIDEOS

The Visionaries Documentary

This video profiles three community mediation programs and a representative case from each – a victim/offender mediation, a race-relations dialogue group, and a multi-party land-use negotiation Produced by PBS, this documentary is an excellent introduction to community mediation for courts, police, and other agencies and groups. VHS approximately 1 hour.

Creating a Safer Community: *Community Mediation and Community Oriented Policing Partnerships*

This video showcases community oriented policing and community mediation center partnerships It identifies the goals and benefits of these partnerships, the use of mediation services conflict management/conflict resolution skills in community oriented policing. Law enforcement personnel, community mediation center staff and community members will find that the video to be a promising resource for community oriented problem-solving. VHS 20 minutes.

Contact NAFCM for price and availability

1527 New Hampshire Ave. NW, Washington DC 20036-1236, USA
www.nafcm.org | nafcm@nafcm.org